THE INCORRECTION

Other Oolichan titles by George McWhirter:

A Staircase for All Souls, 1993
The Book of Contradictions, 2002

THE INCORRECTION

poems

GEORGE
MCWHIRTER

OOLICHAN BOOKS
LANTZVILLE, BRITISH COLUMBIA, CANADA
2007

Library and Archives Canada Cataloguing in Publication

McWhirter, George
The incorrection / George McWhirter.

Poems.
ISBN 978-0-88982-243-6

I. Title.

PS8575.W48I49 2007   C811'.54   C2007-903792-5

We gratefully acknowledge the financial support of the Canada Council for the Arts, the British Columbia Arts Council through the BC Ministry of Tourism, Small Business and Culture, and the Government of Canada through the Book Publishing Industry Development Program, for our publishing activities.

Cover painting by Holly Carr

Published by
Oolichan Books
P.O. Box 10, Lantzville
British Columbia, Canada
V0R 2H0

Printed in Canada on recycled paper

This book is dedicated to
Marina, Lucy and Eva Mairéad

---

*In trying to correct an old wrong
I seem to create a new one
And find myself arraigned
by a hapless incorrection.*

1. FLUID PLACES

(This suite is made up of fey commentary and slender sonnet;
the commentaries, to be read at conversational pace,
more with tongue in cheek than a tear in the eye, and the
slender sonnets, pronounced slowly for the small
syllable music to perform, as best it can
until the water and other matter spill
out of their containment.)

There is a bridge called for Shaw on the Lagan River
that feels to me as though it sits above Belfast,
perhaps, because we used to dive from it,
looking down at the water, and downriver
toward the city, but in that murky flow,
we saw bicycles with buckled wheels
and frames that had been tossed in,
where we shot down to stare at the spokes turn
with a dim glimmer, which made us ponder
for a few breath-deprived moments
on what they would be like
to ride, upside down and underwater,
as if the river were a road
over thin air,
the water and the road rolling over a sky
where there would be no gravity.

Johnny Rodgers, five feet five and Smallman
Mr. Ireland at the time, would suck in his stomach
and inflate his chest—poised on the wall
in his white posing briefs, black-haired,
blue-eyed and as tanned as a splash
of Darjeeling tea, enter
the water.

One day, mangled by middle-age,
he will come back, pectorals
puffy as eyelids, dive and test
the buckled wheels and frame
to take him where—beyond flesh
or gravity, back into his young skin,
looking up from the bottoms
of his plunging eyes at the sky
and my face, looking down for him,

in these lines: black-haired, as blue-eyed
as the sky and Lugh, the Gaelic god
of light, put in a pot of bone and told
to pedal the Lagan with legs of lard
till day breaks out of the East
and the Lough
at its mouth.

A BRIDGE ABOVE STRANMILLIS

I walk on my own
Down a street
Severed by a river
To watch that sweet
Crossroad shiver
Under a halo of stone,
Where a bicycle with one
Wheel is turning on a bed
Stead, a still-to-be-finished
Dream in a pale brown
Brain of water,
A race
Anyone can enter
Without trace.

1. Seaplanes, Sunderland flying boats,
Martin Mars bombers used to be towed,
at a waddle, out of the green hangars
at Jericho, every flying machine
and installation made biblical
by the very name. A tremendous
sheet metal aviary, whose startings-up
and take-offs terrorized,
temporarily, like a convention
of crows, who had forsaken their caw,
to steal
the Rrrrr

        Rrrrrr

           Rrrrrr from the larynx of the lion.

Currently, occupied by a sailing club,
rental Lasers, ocean kayaks, wind
surf boards and sails on the sands
by the pier with its thick green
wrought iron railing.

Behind, backed up against Jericho hill:
Aberthau House, the old officers' mess.
The sky is full of absence, as it always is.
Nothing but air and sea birds—
salt-white flavours of their flight
coasting or curling for the eye
on a saunter
dissolving
* in the sun-yellow evening,*
like the saffron bathed limbs
of a chicken into the stock
for a pot of impeccable
chicken soup.

2. Pet rabbits were released in Jericho Park.
Coyotes came, eagles flew down. Only
the canniest survived to nibble among
the barbed wands of blackberry.

AN ERA OF EASY MEAT AT JERICHO

Where I ramble
By Jericho in the March
Mist and murk to take stock,
I glimpse an eagle perched
On a hemlock,
Above a bramble
Patch and rabbit that cannot dissemble
Its giddy nibbles in the grass, a pet bunny
Its bum left to bob like a yoo-hoo to a tummy
In a tree. Fast food, it will tremble
And jerk, then clog the eagle's throat,
Without redress, like a fur
Coat
On a hamburger.

For some reason it is one of the cleanest beaches. Can it be the Royal Vancouver Yacht club vacuums the Fraser River silt up every morning from around the barques, anchored there for an ungodly sum? In any case, the coliform keeps to either side. Or is it the Folk Fest, the Jazz Fest, or innocence of the Kids' Fest that does not care and knows not how to count the fecal matter? With diapers in play, it ought to rise. Nevertheless, a mystery has been lured into these pale grey waters of the morning, there; much as the spirit of a spring, or a well, might be caught, flirtatiously, in an urn in ancient Macedonia and toted home on some comely lass's shoulder. But even if the water tastes more of river than of sea, its purity is not quite drinkable.

That flavour of fresh water and the man-made lagoon are why mallards and sundry marsh and river birds frequent its reeds and sloping shore. They have the sky and the land to themselves, now that the Sunderlands and Martin Mars are gone.

Ornithologically speaking, anything as stiff-winged as a Sunderland had to be a sitting duck for a sky as yellow as a golden lab, or sun as large as a red retriever dog. There are scads of those.

JERICHO POND

The pink
Swan
Of the sun
Follows
Where duck have swum
Into the wan
Sink
Of evening shallows.
I think
I have gone
From
The bellows
Of the evening dogs with the geese
Into these reedy parentheses.

Every morning on 4th Avenue,
I see the dysphasia of its devotees
Its drinkers—
I almost run them over,
I almost want to,
Almost let myself do it, too,
As they sail out like dozy ghosts
Between the vehicles, to cross
Or stand, staring
Into the whoosh-
Then-by
Gushes
Of traffic
While they swing open their doors,
As though to the other world.

THE DAILY GRAIL

The black host
Can boast
At the surreal
Hilt of the dull
Morning, a bold
Thumb and full
Finger-hold.
On a liquid sword
In the cardboard
Cylinder cup. As if coffee towed
Its horde beyond the balk
Of law, across the road,
Wired, into a rapt J. walk.

To be a bird and fly south,
to know only summer.

We sit in West Point Grey
and watch the birds,
leave an emptiness,
and see geese
give us the V—
like feathered Churchills
as they win over the yielding year
that has put on motley
in the trees, or mufti,
for the fly past.

The only consolation
is that snow may soon do through the eye,
what chocolate does through the mouth,

salve, smooth out
the aggro

but still the tiny dinosaurs above us
who have lost the rulership of the earth
have earned eternal Junes

and the sky
for their concession.

SUNSET: HUATALCO, BAHIAS DE

With a sough and sigh,
Like the belly of a sow
Asleep, the ocean rolls
Over and over on her side.
This is what we call the tide,
The toll
Of water's liquid bell, and now,
The lie
And the lyre
Of dying light,
The grey-blue mire
Has turned into a sty,
A pink eye
Of pure fright.

FROM SOMBRIO
ON VANCOUVER ISLAND: PIGS

I remember always rubbing my eyes and having a sty
on the lid, top or bottom, just at the line of the eyelash—
they would erupt as dry as popcorn
with a pip of yellow butter on top

In the courtyard, between each block
of kitchen houses, pigs were kept
to bring in a little extra bacon
and men would go collecting potato
skins to feed them, or carrot and apple
peel or the tufty top and flaked outer
coat of chopped onions.

        The amalgamated
smell of those leavings was swung
in an enamel bucket, like a censor
down the back streets
by men yowling, "Any auld skins,"
as though the populace had stripped off
their pimply ones, like teenagers,
or mad self-abnegators
in a time of personal plague
too pesky to bear, ready to dump
their marred pelts into the proffered
pig pail.

        From the size and pinkness
of the swine, they could have done, taken up
ownership, put on all the flab of Belfast
on behalf of its citizens.

Those animals shone as big and pink as a sunset
over the Lough, perhaps larger for being there,
in our back brick courtyards.
                    When I run into one—
a sunset—here, at Jericho, I see a fat magenta pig
and if I raise my hand, I truly believe
I might leave a white pock
or dent in its hide
with my finger.

I would
Like to
Leave the green slur
Of love
In this line
On you,
Like the boy
Who left a coy burr
Of robin-
Run-the-hedge
On me and smirked
In passing, all perked
Up, at the edge
Of the wood.

After love, or its making, have you not felt yourself
  squeezed,
like a squid, in the fist of a young fisherman
named José Galindo Montelongo, whose tuna
nets must be cleared of this tentacled
mess by his rubber-gloved hands.

The lamps on the masts and rigging
let his ship pass off Lo de Marco,
on sails of high-intensity
arc light, as astonishing
as our own faces
in the glare of bedside halogens

casting for those depth-charges
of passion that only splash
and plunge into us
after dark
            as unbidden,
as the albacore.

On TV, in clubs, in movie
houses it plays over
and over. Under the lights,
as the people power-fish for it;
on decks and in vessels rigged
with strobe and spots,

they sail in parallel
after these bombs,
this torpedo of meat. Its steak
is like rounds of a tree, readable,
edible eternity in the mouth,
as whorled and as thick
as love.

THE TUNA

is a bomb of a body
with fins
tiny as robins'
wings. What shoddy
fortune our a-
ppetite makes of an
ocean
bird, whose song
is speed; its blue gong
under the boat and silver
bleep squeaks
by in a nightly throng
of phosphor.

Beware if you go
dolphin or whale
watching, here.

In Brazil, they say
boto, the dolphin-man,
never takes off his hat
to make love. He does
his naked hat dance
between your thighs,
tips it when he's done
and frolics off
into the surf, hat
on head, like those
women through the high hills
and vales of Bolivia.

Don't be afraid
if you see him in a shop,
trading his old fedora
for something new
to cover his blow hole.

He is too troubled
with counting the cost
to wet your whiskers
with a drop of love
and lure you
like the miniature
catfish at the pet shop
into his saucer
of sea water.

TANGOLUNDA*

A thin Tilly-hatted
Man tip-toes
By, as if the immaculate
Wet
Sneakers he holds, elbows
Delicately bent,
Were rotted
Fish.
I have kept this wish
Redolent
Into old age, a recipe
Of love for you so ripe—Eee,
It has my nose
In throes.

*Tangolunda means *beautiful woman* in Zapotec

Ask and it shall be given thee . . . knock and it will be
opened onto thee was too easy and obvious
for me to get the hang of, and forward, onward,
the command—as into battle, like Christian Soldiers—
although I had to sing the hymn and repeat its summonings
at every session of the McComb Memorial, Junior L. O. L.
always baffled my urge for the reverse.

Later, if my own sideways and evasive
approach to the breast
and belly of the wonderful, the omphalos
of all loveliness, had held sway,
coitus would have been complete
the moment Angela's and my hips met,
in passing, pollinating
by pure proximity of pores.

Scented side orders of sex,
not chips, would have been my teenage
craving of choice. Since nothing of importance
happened to me directly,
and always to the side, escaping
around the corner of my eye
I set a convex course.

Hard to be permanently headed
around the corner of one's eye!
Hard to live with, but you have . . .
front and side,
                    since you first
made me turn and turn
                    glazed donuts
for your favour, while you laid
unpronounceable ratatouille

and potato casseroles
before me and said eat.
                              What outlandish
treats to set before the Irish king
of procrastinating,

who, way back then, and oddly,
ate in English only.

CRABBING

finally I nab and chuckle
at the dubious logic
of the crabs. Like sick
belt buckles,
gone mad & AWOL
from their straps—
with no real lateral
release, they dodge
to, and from their bondage:
two overlapping traps
of land and sea. Thus do
the sand pants snap
off the tide and fall,
repeatedly, in situ.

Sproat Lake has a hydrology so rapid
it rehydrates, its body of water entirely replaced
and replenished, every four years.
Now, taking a leap year and a jug of Sproat Lake H20
from one, and another from the next, then a sip
from each, one is assured of never having drunk
the same water twice, which extends the maxim
of Heraclitus, by way of time-lapse experiment
to standing bodies of water into which
most streams do pour.

Little grows there, and fish don't go there
but one can drink and swim
in its reputed
and repeated
freshness.

The raw carrot is not
Just a puritan's orange
That keeps its juice
Uptight—yon citrus blot,
That rumpled nuisance,
Rolls down its pyramids
Like a drunk—risible
Bldg material next stock piles,
Vitamin A caryatids
Of the eye—visible
Like earth's missiles
Plumed, each in its silo
Ready to level the angio
After the big binge.

The ache
in the Falls Road
and Belfast Corporation
Baths, or at Pickie's
(by the seaside)
Pool, as our eyes baked
in salt
and poorly dilu-
ted chlorine

like live
anchovy
in our heads!

When we came out
we cried solid
chemical
through the chill
titrations
of the wind
and air.

Now, with snug,
plug-
perfect goggles
on their insightful
sockets,
and the generosity
of Johnson's
Baby Shampoo,
there'll be no
more tears
in our kids' eyes
after their bath.

POOL

In a sweat, past hot bricks
In the wake of summer
A mum and son swimmer.
Legs, tapered into tallow wicks,
Wiggle on 4 scant ankles
And splayed feet, skin—a thin
Tan that rankles
With chlorine. Heart of a leviathan
In the aqua halls, will he hum
The national anthem, will they calve
There for him on the podium
As they did for her, the torrid tears
Soldering her cheeks, the salt salver
That would flavour her years?

Water has more disguises than anything, more apparel and appearances than any woman, but is still thought of as an element. We might readily reduce anything we wish to its core of water. We say people are this or that of the first water. It is primary and salubrious. My mouth mines for it in every vegetable with its mineral additions and deceptions. What fools me I call food. To enter the waterway of any legume or tuber, the carrot—if you will, is to navigate the long, tapered, orange canals on Mars. Those are our proper destinations, our future seas, the fat, purple-coated, green-capped oceans of eggplant. For admission, like Franklin, all we need do is die, but instead of applying through a furrow of ice, we need simply get dug into a garden.

SOUND BYTE

The delicate
Ribs
Of celery
With eeri-
Er tail jibs
And spate
Of brittle
Water,
Like spittle
Or a disor-
Dered pale green sea
Inside the liquid
Lining of what I see
Is my third eyelid.

In the rain
It dangles, turned
Into jewellery
That devours the entrails
Of everything small with wings
That is attracted to it . . .
                    But can it
Actually stay sticky enough—
Will the sliding threads
And clinging beads
Of rain not dilute
The abdominal
Glues?   This
Is my question
For CBC's Quirks
And Quarks.

DAY 100 OF THE SPIDER'S DIET

Why should I not clone
you these amethysts,
walking on their own
necklaces, hung from twists
of pipe and the corrugated jowls
of gutters. I gripe, eat bowls
of porridge to hew
down the tummy, but how late
must I wait to eat your plate
of tofu-
burger when I feel as cannibal
a scribe of the sarcophagal
as these erratic amber dolmen
with mulatto abdomen?

Since I grew up,
            looking out to sea, across at some spot
between Ireland and Scotland, at Ilsa Craig and Iona,
 where Irish monks hid and did their considerable
and difficult washing after the dissolution of their loose,
and native monastic habits by the hierarchy
in Rome,
            I believed I had my vision
and needed no more: I would be a bachelor
and wash my own clothes while staring at,
or fishing in the ocean for my fodder.

            So then, how is it
that I looked down on myself diving
for a wedding ring
into the seaweeds at Millisle,
                        in water
as clear as a glacier's?
                        Well you may ask!
A Johnny Rodgers of the mind, a small
man's Mr. Intellect I was to be, poised
in my posing pants, diving for ideas
till my dying day.

                        That was the way I saw it—
off, into a Lough and Lagan
of rippling little lyrics, immortalized by liquid
alliterations,
            but as vast and moving as the view
from our small sea windows,
                        my square portholes.
which well describes my queerness of eye

before it was made round for me by a woman,

in order to admit the shape of the world:
                         a woman's,
from where I see it, now,
              if one regards the curves
of North and South America as such:
        our God,
            the cartographer's

                              Venus.

THAT JULY

if you had biffed her
in her mules, sham
patterned stockings of rain
teeming down; her leg
not fat as a keg
nor thin-stemmed
as a champagne snifter,
but sloped as a boor's
delight in a Crown
lager sleeve, as pro tem—
the skin, light-brown
and drinkable. No truer
way to follow the sun
than the tan to her bum.

One takes mining to favour a tier of precious metals:
  veins of gold at the top
for random, then concerted extraction—early peoples
  stumbled and fumbled
upon some, then dug for more—off the halo of deposits
  or metallurgical bow
laid, as we learned from Mr. Smith in Geography, by
  the crude
smelter of the molten globe; base metals—copper, nickel,
  lead—settled deeper
in the subterraneous pecking or picking order. Mr.
  Smith's hierarchical arc
of metals fascinated me, and when John, a geologist
  friend turned litterateur,
told me of a company he formerly worked for buying a
  licence and rights
over a sweep of sea floor to prospect for ocean placers, I
  wasn't disabused
of the natural order among minerals and metals. John's
  former company
also secured rights to contiguous resources
on the sea floor—shell fish, sand and gravel, the latter
  mineral
worth more than any metal to mining.

"But how?"

"It's sunk into everything that keeps a city standing.
Concrete, dummy! Pavement. You'd still be hauling your
  butt through mud
like a caveman if it wasn't for sand and gravel." Then, he
  informed,

I should bless the sand and gravel wrapped around our
  drain tile
for my nice dry basement.

"What's that cost, what's that worth
compared to the entire sum of gold in your household"

"We only have two wedding rings . . . so," I surmise
  further, "the prospective
Placer Gold Co. turned to gravel
when it found none of the incorruptible in the ocean?"

"No, they stumbled on a scallop bed in the place
of the placers and the outfit did a quick change
to a scallop fishery. Very compatible
dredge and shuck operation . . . like mining
live platinum in a shell. Chalk that up
to the miracle of those creatures who do double
geological and genetic duty, the fossil rock
from which the living make a nifty living
off their futures as fine dining,
not chalk or limestone."

"What do you call that?" I ask the gleam in John's eye.

"I would say a timely and timeless
liquid asset."

44

WEE BOYS AT CARNALEA STATION

A tunnel
Under the rail-
Lines poses
A black blossom
For our mine/ors' noses.
The glum knell
And trickle
Of water is our
Cathedral.
Dower,
Ankle-deep glitter
Of liquid coal.
Juvescent fossils, we gleam
In the seam of the stream.

The layer of slate slid down like a ship, keel up, into the ground. Before there was ground. Over a block of old granite. A plug of it, or gargantuan boulder, leaving a gap at sea level. At least, sea level in the time ice melted and the water rose. Like my straight ruler laid over my bent knuckle on the desk in Geography. Logic dictates the gap for the cave runs the length of the soft gap in the granite knuckle. Not long, but enough.

A thing for me to think about in class—the chink. All that's left of the cave, whose floor is packed with smooth sea stones.

My mind mines the opening. Did the sea or contrabanders fill the cave with the stones because the tide doesn't reach and cloak the cavity any more?

Remove the stones and they would make a pile visible to the shore walk and require a night and day watch—if there were a box or a vault for storing gold or two-hundred-year-old brandy in there. If it's not gold, I'm too young to drink and I'm revolted by the taste when my uncle gives me a sip, before he sinks it in the hot milk for his toddy.

After I tell him, for he's the only one who'll see the value in it, my uncle takes his dream of contraband brandy to bed with him. A brigantine, barrels of Napoleon brandy rolling like wooden boulders in the hold, invades his horizon.

And mine, has my uncle down by the water, now, in his striped green and gold pyjamas, signalling, wrapping up stones from the cave in the thin leather ribbons of his fingers to remove the stones and make room for the drunkenness of duty free to come. Erin gebrach.

It's crushing to go with that cache into French.

This morning I saw frost break into a beaded sweat
on the holly leaves and stipple-lacquer
their intense green. The sky was true-blue too, yet
of such fine omens I have always been a mocker,
and of your face, which only a poltroon—
me—would razz, for fear of an inadequate
love song. I am the seagull set to croon
from the rooftop, but who may only grate,
a blank-breasted admiral on yellow feet,
across the asphalt shingle with an unmusical
command, whose notes are neither rare nor fleet
but whose wings, when he dives, beat our street
into a fjord, an air as stinging as Chablis, an untypical
perspective to flow from this flying madrigal.

AFTER MELVILLE

For simplicity, let's say the forest is divided between
the squirrels and the eagles, bears and beavers,
cougars, and ants who in summertime also ranch
on cabbage leaves and milk the aphids
in my wife's garden.
The sea divides the same,
into fish, mammals, crustaceans and amphibians,
and the water is its own home and forage,
no vegetable growth like the forest,
but a flowing element, grower and destroyer;
it works off the moon and wind, the highs
and lows of the air,
and if I were to look down
upon the dry land hemisphere
as I look down upon the sea,
only the streaming air
and sky would be visible, and the birds—
all the rest that scrawl and crawl below the foliage,
crab and lobster-like—
gorillas under their banana fronds, bull elephants
beneath the acacia and the flame tree,
cows in the grass, and cockroaches everywhere—
unobservable, until the latter
(or they all) take flight.
Of the ocean woods, seaweeds and their industries,
I know little and little more about what creatures
graze while others predate, what plant phenomena
what seeds and pollens sew the foliage of sea to sea
the way birds' wings, air currents and winds carry
the germination between the dry-land continents.
These underwater fomentations
persist, a matter of my ignorance.

Planktons I know are edible, alive
and swimming; and various whales—
like sieves, their giant metropoli
of blubber puff and blow
around clouds of motes and light that synthesize
into food, the protozoa converting the eater
through communion
into an ocean follower.
Mounted on such high, sea-horsed notions,
which often break
into a liquid gallop,
a longing takes me across the Pacific,
north to South Seas, where once in a lagoon,
on Upolu, I saw an eye
in the ocean watch me,
and I must make account of it— as Ishmael,
or Bartelby, the scrivener, might with his quill.
In a henge of coral obelisks:
there was one like a solid, furry brown brain,
and the other equally mossy, but long-stemmed,
an orb of symmetrical antennae
for the workings of calcium mind
within the un-drawn sphere of its circumference
I confess I hung over it, a chandelier of loose
white flesh and predator of the peculiar,
tracking its thinking parts: tiny, electric blue
twitches that disappeared, as if the stone
had had a different idea, been taken aback
enough to withhold something brilliant.
I hung there, playing drifter,
sea-cowpoke, shedding the light of my skin
on their absence until they came, one brief query
after another, then teeming up to my tummy
from all around the stems of proto-conscious

coral, now completed by electric blue dots
into an identifiable orb, or an iris
attached to the myriad rods of its eye
fixed on my umbilicus,
and my face, with a spout in its mouth.
What are we doing here? they asked.

I will make a sonnet
Of a grape, leaving the tentacular
Love of the vine, a damask
Sheet, pegged spectacular
To the line, or flask
Of sea from the Inlet;
Once your lips are wet
With these syllables,
You have drunk it;
And in Sawyer's, the fishmonger's,
I have been lined up for a rabbit
Since 1944, ready to grab it
By the feet, to feed a hunger
As quick as you, and unbelievable.

> *Love took me*
> *To a strange South Sea island*
> *Which I had never been to*
> *Before but had never left*

In Ed's Linen, the Greek store clerk listens to us rave about our discovery of persimmon. We describe the fruit with the ruff, the wide frilly hard grey collar around the top, like a pumpkin—colour of a pumpkin. "I know the fruit you mean," she says.

"We call it Lotos."

"Lotus?" says I, sincerely fuddled.

"What the lady give Odysseus so he stay on that island," the Ed's Linen clerk adds.

Fuddled further, I fumble for my first tongue test, the crack of hard wax skin, the softening and spread of subtle juice, which is as much made of me as it.

As two people mulling love into a distinctiveness, the soft stinging, clinging sweetness of saliva, as when a man, Odysseus or I, takes back his tongue from a fragrant mouth.

I am looking up into the persimmon tree on Blanca, or pua in Samoa, which the woman of my life takes me under to look into the arc of green, heavily folded

petals, the fruit with the fairy collars and the blush, demurely cloaked, but still obtruding visibly, assuredly, as if already in bed with you, ready to be eaten, its collar taken off, while imperceptibly inside memory and forgetting perspire in a sugary glaze.

My son says "It's too like a hard tomato."

"A wax tomato?" I define it to myself in Ed's Linen.

But with a hint of yam in its eventual yumminess, if we are talking fruity vegetables. The persimmon has a migrant taste, a queer encompassing of orient and oc-

*cident, a lichee to the salal savour in its globe, a caramel
simmered sap of a woman under the flesh, which is hard
at first for a man to get through, before it haunts and
changes how he views the world as this one fruit, whose
flavour memory has assumed and been consumed by for-
ever, as I am by one woman, my lotus and my flower who
leads me into much reflection in her long enthralling; my
vision, living on this lens of liquid, which is ground into
something perfect and lucid by the earth and rains un-
der the cinnamon soils of an island,*

>*its water mantle sweetening the salt of the
>lagoon's kisses around my shoulders
>Or under the low leaves and branches of the
>persimmon tree on Blanca,
>atop its hill
>above the beach of silk-silt
>loomed by the rain and the great river
>flowing from the enchanted forest, here, in the
>Northwest.
>Even if the lotus is not a persimmon,
>I could believe her, the Greek store clerk in Ed's Linen.*

THE IONAN

Catholic to the core,
But no lover of Rome
Heretofore,
On his island home
With his pole, the tense
String and bob
Of his persistence,
Fishing for redemption,
Not fish, the gob
Of God to bite on
The twine
And bless
The loneliness
Of his line.

2. EPICURIOSITIES & PO-ESSAYS
FROM THE DAILIES

The dailies, the weeklies, the fortnightlies, the monthlies . . .
resist what you're
thinking—the old dirty word-
play, it stands for incorrection.

THE TALE OF THE DONKEY

THE NEW YORK TIMES, Monday February 27th, 2006, Marilise Simons in "Marrakech Journal; Keeping the Moroccan Tradition Alive, One Tale at a Time" quotes Juan Goytisolo, an eminent Spanish writer living in that country, who remembers 'Sarouh, a strongman and tale spinner, who would lift a donkey into the air in Jemaa el Fna, the main square of Marrakech for traders, storytellers and performers. The donkey would begin braying, and as people came running, "You fools," Sarouh would yell at the crowd. "When I speak about the Koran, nobody listens, but all of you rush to listen to a donkey.'"

I can hear the same bray and snort,
at the curve, bottom of the hill
up Northumberland Street in Belfast,
where the Great Northern Flax
& Spinning Mill girls tossed toe
at me on their lunch hours—
a uniformed mule,

stubbornly pursuing his way
with a bale of books on his back,

on the same curve where my father
lifted the donkey in his story
when it refused the hill, and later,
growing in size to a mule,
then a horse as the ire
and eye of his memory
inflated its weight
and proportions.

There is no doubt he carried the beast,
my mother confirms, and lets
him stew in the predicament
of his tale, how to get it up the hill.

He had been hiding from her—
mad, anti-Papish, McConnell woman—
down the Falls, smoking, lighting
his cigarettes with the rest
off the candles under the Sacred Hearts

—off the shame burning in Jesus's breast
for him. Not selling a thing,
just letting them steal him blind
off the cart. Hardly enough apples left
to bribe the donkey back home.

So, he lost his rag. Got it from between
the shafts of the cart, told the donkey
it was an ass and a disgrace
and was getting one last chance—
it could run to hell or stay and pull the cart.
The donkey did neither; it just stood its ground
and he got under, took it on his shoulders
and holding out his elbows, to keep the beast
in place, laid either hand on a shaft

and hefted. "Bloody madmen, what they'll
do for a fag," my mother said. "They'd steal
the job off a donkey. She was implying
mad, as in dumb, addicted Irish—
which he was.

And I followed him down Northumberland Street,
on my way through the Falls
to the school of fools

and storytellers, stealing my job
off a donkey, or a mule, or a horse
whatever I can grab to carry an audience
along with.

MURAL

Installation artist, Gu Wenda, conceives The Great
Wall as being built of hair bricks,
the sun-kilned heads of labourers who hauled them
on the bone huds of their clavicles and shoulders.
Stacked in trays for Gu Wenda's brickworks exhibition,
as always, the bricks resemble loaves,
but in a gory bakery of desiccated brains,
not grains.

The New York Times commentator on the art,
Sheldon Melvin, says that a curtain of hair
by the same Gu Wenda is as inexplicably beautiful
as his hair bricks are dour and disturbing.
Old China was a walled world of courtyards and cities,
like Mexico and Spain, or Roman Britain,
any place with its back to the barbarians—
from Picts to the Mongol Hordes, and bricks
have been the daily bread of slavery—
from the time of the Middle-Kingdom Ming
to Moses in Egypt they stand
in the mortar of memory,
monumentally.

In the same life-threatened light, I once translated
a section of the Mexican poet, Jose Emilio Pacheco's
poem, "Tree Between Two Walls," adding mine
to the bigger portion by Edward Dorn
and Gordon Brotherston in a New Directions book.
This particular threat to trees does not exist
in our experience here: the encroachment upon
and incarceration of the natural by walls;
the vision of the tyrannized tree is reversed
across our lane every day
in this leafy otherland,

oaks, which JC Carolan planted
out of nostalgia for his native Boston,
send helicopter fruit down the boulevard
on twirling green blades to lock into the grass
good neighbour Sergeant Fru wanted bare of trees.
so kids could play
baseball, football, basketball, unimpeded,
over his sweep of personally policed
lawn. His 4600 Block front yards and our kids
never knew a wall as they were growing up—
until Mexico, where we trailed them with us
while I translated "A Tree Between Two Walls"
into reality along the adobe or raw, brick-walled
walks of Cuautla whose walls followed
every wrinkle in the hills
through that part of Morelos.

Meanwhile, in that same era
across our back lane, a volunteer alder
intervened between the gables of 4636
and 4638 West 12th, joining an insurgency
with Casimir's live Christmas tree,

three lots away on our side of the lane
(now thirty feet tall and as many yuletides on),
to topple any stucco establishment, adjacent
or adjoining our side in this brief dynasty of dwellings,
whose millennia lie only in the numbers on our doors.

THE RESISTANCE MOVEMENT

*Reeds plucked from the Midi fields
and sharpened into pens that only held
a little ink for the quick strokes
of van Gogh drawing,

If the birds in our garden of the 13th Avenue West
had drops of ink in their beaks,
would they sketch the design in which they toil not
and neither do they sew
until my love and I learn there is no real labour in a job
with a sun clock and food growing in the ground for free,
all about us, to be harvested by our eyes.

This is what van Gogh would never recover from:
the old Abbey on Montmajour, the frenzy of incitement,
competing with God in his work,
with the visible notes of a pen
he could never inquill the sway of reeds,
    of true bristle bloom
and the pom-poms at their ends like jesters',
in a field of Provènce

while he lived. He could only do it in the resistance,
by working through the plum underground
job of his grave.

*from Michael Kimmelman's Art Review, WEEKEND ARTS,
The New York Times, October 14, 2000

Picking salal leaves for crèches, wreaths and floral
arrangements has put a severe strain upon the plant's
survival and it should be placed on the endangered list.

To the salal (Gaultheria Shallon) berry
I owe this apologia—
to you, the edibles of the bush,
who hang in slack bags or tight pods
     of black porridge
                (dark podge, star
                    /stodge
                    /gleam)
in the umber of the forest,
under the gloss of the leaf, the verdiglaze.
        What a dull jam your berries
bubble into—an overly dun poi
Hawaiians would appreciate, be made
peaceable and at home by,
had they ever come paddling by these beachheads
with the beaks of thunderbirds
and maw of every bear on every totem
aimed their way.
Or would you be confitured,
        poor berry,
        fed as syrup and dried cake?

        I am afraid
I don't eat you happily and can't quite like
those few handfuls I pick close to home.
To be honest, most favour the verdiglaze,
the precious gloss of the leaf for a crèche
or Christmas wreath, or bold natural bouquet
and floral display. Like so many, many things,
your talented plant can survive obscurity
but not a surplus
of appreciation,

the aesthetic value. For this
your bush is over-harvested
and you are put in danger of extinction.

If it were just you, who were simply eaten,
the world of salal might go on ad infinitum—
you, the fruit, being the sacrifice,
fat little black-faced Jesus, saviour of the bush.
Why do I not eat, then, but let my taste collude
in a holocaust, which ends the life
of your entire genus to turn you into a living-room
artefact?

I confess I haven't told you all. I did disdain—
until I nibbled on a number
beside the blueberries on a mountain top,
after you had been winter-cured,
prepped under metres of snow and clean rain,
I misprized and I misappraised
until I spied the blue taste of you
that sizzled under pot holes in the snow
and savoured your small drizzle of the celestial
on my tongue.

I apologize. I have eaten you from sour ground,
too close to a swamp and the city.
I apologize for calling you podge,
dull porridge, overly dun poi, and grovel
o'er your black chalice as my just dessert.

ON THE NORTH SOUTH ROAD

Korean kids, Grade Sevens,
go wide-eyed in gleeful wonder
at the idea of spies and tanks'
steel caterpillar treads
chewing twelve miles of asphalt
down the road to Seoul
from the North Korean border.
The blocks built to explode
over the road, in that eventuality,
turn the monolith from simple blocks,
which can be bypassed,
into a permanent blockade; the real
hindrance, however, is
that the North has no political machinery
that can trundle thus far South
under the treads of Kim Il Sung's
ideologueology.
So, the kids maintain
an absolute disbelief
in any mobilized Northern
nuttiness and think ipods
will fix and tune the North's
deaf ears in
to what really rocks.
The South Korean Seventh Graders say, I quote—
It sounds like a story from faraway,
and the automatic translator in me
suspects the reporter
feeding the story to *The New York Times*
meant far-fetched.
Old gods and engines
of war outlive their warranties
when no one gives them credence,
except at that moment

when, like a giant star,
they are about to expire
and the excitement and awe
they once incited
goes nova
as it did with us.

ON A ROAD THROUGH WEST BELFAST

Protestants, incensed at the lapsed vigilance
and Popery creeping in
under the banner of human rights,
burst into a beetroot red and black
pudding of anger
around their big jawed Pastor's
well-boiled abhorrence on the rotunda
outside the Stadium Picture house
at the top of the Shankill; the mob
rolled down the road
and put in the windows of the Italian
ice cream shops (the Italians',
who had fled blue-jawed
Mussolini)—they
being the only Papists
the Prods could find.

Black holes in the human
heart and head
             (little studied)
that compound
in the implosion of belief—once its positive
light dies, the negative takes a quantum
leap to unstoppable power and intensity
to the point of no return and no surrender.

                Let old blocks
stay on the road to Seoul, inscrutably
doing what is forgotten
for the kids to marvel at. They laid
no such mysteries to posterity
on the Shankill.

CORN

In Ralston, Iowa, the surplus
corn, 2.7 billion bushels
piles 60 feet high* in a pyramid
of cobs and kernels that gleam
like nuggets still intact
in a spill of maize ingots
from the bullion farms,
and worth their weight in the gold
of U. S. subsidies to the farmers.
Sir Robert Peel, that misunderstood man,
tried to quell a famine by adding
subsidized corn to the Irish diet.
"Food for horses," they said,
like someone else claimed
German was a language fit
for horses. Both were wrong.
Had they developed a taste for it
(corn and the language for horses)
there may have been no world wars
with capital letters and numbers
and no Great Hunger with any upper case to it
If the authorities were just to truck that corn
to the poor and hungry of the hurricane.
in Louisiana . . . ! But alas, no electric or gas
to boil it or butane turns out to be
too pricey to turn on. Ah the poor authorities
who giveth here only what they taketh away there,
perpetually Peter-Pauling, always looking at a fine
fix for the constant craving or the raving, like a junkie
unable to find a clean unabused entry point
to deliver the stuff,
an uncorrupted spot on the map to insert the needle.

*Alexei Barrionuevo article, *New York Times*, page 1, Wednesday,
November 9, 2005

ELMS

Elms, along the boulevard
with deep vertical grooves in the bark,
then oak, with a smoother, almost ruddy
vein through the trunk,
you are picking up *The New York Times*,
free faculty and student
summer edition, thinking of the bark
on trees as skin while you read
how they lay the skin of unborn babies
on babes, flesh of the unwanted
on the beloved, and it joins, becomes
what it never could be, alive and
growing into a boy or girl
as their own flesh
which will suffer cuts and bruises
beyond these colossal burns
on which a patch of embryo
was laid, like a poultice—a monstrous thing
to heal a monster child whose face
may have creaked before,
as it smiled, painfully,
anticipating another graft to replace the old one
that would not grow, never become them—
their own Frankenstein skin,
butchered neatly from a buttock,
placed cheek to cheek, as it were,
fruitlessly, for life.

When the eyes crinkle
in the park light under the elms,
when you stoop and look up at
your own lately-grafted children,
racing away over the playground into the swings,
glowing with the latest in cell technology—

the age in their face is living,
still growing, not arrested like an old graft
would be, or the foetus was, in biological
time.

An elm can grow an elm from an elm,
if we need it to, thicken and twist up into grooves
 deep enough to swallow the tips of our finger.
We love its coarse ugliness.
but the new way of the baby
Saint Frankenstein's skin through the park
your child might wear now
if its face fell in the fire
when you weren't looking, or it tipped
through the hot, open door of the oven
when it peered or leaned in too far
to examine a pie,
or its hand picked up
a pot, too hot to hold, like this paradox
of the flesh that shocks. However you feel
about that—your child should shake hands
and feel the lasting friendship
happen through someone else's hand. Under every elm
or oak on the way, shake hands. Smile,
press the flesh for two
in the one skin. Your child is their only
contact with the living.

ON SENDING OUT OUR KIDS AGAIN*

"Sugar and spite
make everything night."

Why should we dress them up
and send them out on a Halloween
Sunday, or any other day?

Why should we lay the inverted barnacles
of our children's ears on the rock of ages
to be smashed?

                    Be it
the sober grey serge
                    of Presbyterian granite. Or Jesuit
obsidian. Or pure Koranic chalk, made from the snow
of protozoa in the Persian Gulf.
                    Or basalt that seeps—to my
Ulster eye—like O'Neil's blood into the slim strands
of Strangford Lough,
           as rag-endy
                    as the wrist he slashed off
and the hand he flung like a son
ahead of him to touch shore first, telling all
of his immortal will to win
over a Scottish giant
in this wee wager
of an ocean race.
                    But what can the astonished
gashes of our children's mouths report, but burial?
The gags
are these gross convulsions of folded stone
that resemble us in bed,
                    which must play
their hard copulations backwards

at minus ten billion motions
to the moment
to get hot
with the engendering
again.
                  The smile crossing
our children's faces is the cosmic splash, the hit movie
we have waited all of time for at the box-office,
the blockbuster in the Hollywood
on Broadway.

                  These dimpled chins
are not made to be our animated glyphs,
our impertinent messages written
                              into their infant skin
for God, but God's kisses
                  turned into lips that wet our cheeks.
Waddling, falling, gasping, snuffling,
                              they come asking us
to wipe their noses, change
their sodden socks, un-mummify
them from their muddy-buddies.
                  Let us get up off our asses
                  and our knees. Find baby Buddha,
Jesus and Mohammed their Huggies.
Stop stuffing their genitals
with gelignite, sending them out
into the street,
                  to knock on our neighbours' doors,
begging for a fistful
                              of poisoned
Halloween candies
to make their visit worthwhile.

*A response to Karen Cooper's essay on "Of Inca Sacrifice Found
Frozen in Time" by Johan Reinhard, photographs by Maria Stenzal,
Vol 196, No. 5, *NATIONAL GEOGRAPHIC*, November 1999

TO A T

" . . . federal aid to farmers in all its myriad forms: crop-insurance programmes, set asides, payments-in-kind, marketing loans, export subsidies, flood-control benefits and, valiable above all in the Californian cotton fields, where it takes 257 gallons of water to grow a T-shirt, cheap irrigation water."

—From "Cottonocracy," *THE ECONOMIST*, October 18th, 2003.

"It takes 257 gallons of water to grow a T-shirt in California," which makes two people, say, a father and a mother standing in a yard, in theirs, equal to a large emergency sump or cistern of H2O.

The full measure for a family of four would drain a duck or big garden pond, two bare-bottomed lovers, doing it with their T-shirts on would fill more than the volume of the bath they share, before they get in.

A crowd at a company retreat, roaring their pep-slogan and T-shirted in its logo is a cloud-burst, a desiccated flood. At any one time of any day, the population of any large city becomes a summer sea, an evapo-morphic Gulf Stream or Humboldt Current, synthesised into cotton or other textile

combinations. How many gallons of water does it take to grow a long sleeved shirt? To get it from Mr. Jim Boswell, the grower in California, Calvin Klein et al must truck a waterfall in and out of the textile factory. In (terms of standing water) our beloved T-shirt, when we pull it on, we are aiding and abetting an aqueduct, an aquecide; we are the legs that walk under the dark water tower in the desert and drain it

to fill this two, chopped-arm and single-torso temple
of sacrifice to a casual,

sartorial, no-necked effigy.

Every time you see rain pass over California, it is a T-
shirtinthemaking,andsocooltowearbeforeanyoneelse,
so get out and try it on before it ever hits the bloom or
the loom. Really, you'll find it even cooler than cotton.

AMAZONIAN TRIPTYCH

1

Rosewood oil of the Amazon
in my soap
makes me feel beautiful and sad
as the Lady of Shallot
towering
at her loom of loveliness
with its deadly needle
which doesn't kill me,
but the tree
in the faraway factory of oil,
where its trunk is milled into a liquid
guarantee of scent
that will make men sniff
and look up at me
as at the vanished rosewood
from the Amazon.

2

On the flanks of that forest,
trunks rise like pipelines to the sky,
swerving in the eye wherever it might look up
the green telescope of bark or into the ghost
spectrometer of leaves that twinkle greenly
with the rosé squint of sunlight
over the haunches of a cow, and the clap it drops
like a stinking leaf on the pasture. These four-legged
fauna grow flora that is unsmokeable
and cannot be stirred into a mildly
extra-sensory tea, such as *hierba maté*,
but we sup it up in another incarnation—the cow curd,
for it serves as soy-burger helper to the beans

through the promotion of growth, and the patties
sit, remarkably,
      like the smaller simulacra
of cow pie
   on the plate. No bones
about it.

CLAP

Many of the extra cows are grazing on land that was once rainforest often illegally occupied rather than bought. Some pasture land is later used to grow Soya, another commodity with a Variations international market. The ranchers move deeper into the forest.

—From "The Price of Success,"
THE ECONOMIST, April 17th – 23rd, 2004

The cowpat on the crop of soy was once a tree,
axe-harvested (along with many creatures,
who feasted on the leaves and fungi close by)
in order to let soy supply vegans protein in the far-away,
after the meat-eaters have had their dibs at bully beef
and beef dip from Brazil.
     Sip *yerba maté*
and ruminate on the tree that made it,
the twigs and leaves dried to pewter-coloured pieces,
or the clay-grey of dry gumbo
with which some paint their kitchen walls
into a tasteful neutrality. These twigs and leaves
are kept alive as fine-food factories, and perhaps
that sort of sylvan machinery is fine, its sap
as truly rechargeable as a cold-fusion
battery. The cerebral window-wiper of the mate
almost lets one see the whole soy-paradox, planted
like a magic beanstalk, whose tips reach into a heaven
that feeds the conscience of the chosen: we choosier-
than-thou's in the North, who look down
with extensile, ambiguous eyes
at the cowboys and CJD-free cattle that graze, methodically,
and do not stagger, yet. There is fungal magic also
to topple our senses and our qualms,
in the wild new crop of mushrooms—the morels,
thickening like edible aces of spades, or clusters

of brown scar tissue in the hands of the pickers,
which inspires a hungry empathy
for the morel's sultry, wounded flavour, only able
to flourish after slash and burn?
How profligate, after the scourge of fire, the soy bean
and the manna of morels, these endless post scriptum
in the volume of Amazonian life.

BATS

For José Emilio Pacheco

"*Bats and agriculture*: Fear Vandals,
not vampires"
—*THE ECONOMIST*, January 6th, 2007

They are building a bridge for the bats,
(bats being among the bridge's most favoured,
future users) with crevices, carefully bat-sized
and right cozy roosts, so the free-tailed bats
can work the graveyard shift,
eating pink boll worm,
aka the corn earworm,
saving ten bolls, or two cents worth of cotton
on every night-flight
tour of duty,
preening the crops. As rent
that translates into sixty-two cents a month—cheapest
accommodation a bat could find.

There are pallid bats and big brown bats in California,
much like the people, and between their bat wings
that flicker like flames of black silk through the dark,
their mouths consume moths and beetles
with the minutest crackle—the way movie stars
dispose of letters by fans, drawn to write and mail
them their humble, pen-and-paper, insect love.

In Mexico they dynamite the free-tails' caves,
to cut off the carriers of rabies. from flying free at night,
to seal the bloodsucking mouths inside the hills,
but those fur-collared and leather-jacketed
aviators are hooked on the agave

flowers, not tequila drinkers' throats, which will run dry
with no bat-pollination for their supplies.

Like shooting bees off the vine, all spring and summer,
then going to the gates of a winery in the fall,
still expecting to hear the clink of bottles
on trucks headed for the rail head.

Those free-tails—who winter south of the Rio Grande
on an exchange program of migrant labour

for
    twenty Mexican centavos a night,
or
    forty-seven pesos, eighty centavos

below Mexican minimum* wage, a real
steal for South of the Border. Don't shoot,
chop, poison or blow
them up—

    let them work in the dark

for next to nothing
if they want.

---

*In Mexico, at this date, minimum wage is 48 pesos per day,
which is about $4. 00 U. S or $4. 80 Canadian

MISSED MANNERS

Science & Technology
Eye on the storm
—*THE ECONOMIST,* Feb 24th 2000

The soul of politeness
no longer allows his breath
to cool his soup
in case it blow up
into a Hurricane Katrina spray
over his spouse or son. He winces
until she raises and pours his noodles and broth
over and off his spoon to cool, instead,
moving the chicken soup as a dredger does
the silt of a yellow river.

He reads heated water rises
like the retina of a hurricane's eye
in the Gulf of Mexico,
an oval of potential malevolence,
the same as on the spoon

around the Coca and the Loca currents
of a conversation.

Such gravity there is
at the luncheon table
that can go either way.

One lunch time,
trapped in its
own escalated convection,
it may fly around the yelling
and the yellow
chicken noodle soup in the bowl,

and jolt
straight up, instead of falling,
the counter-gravity
of it
like the poltergeist impulse
    of all dark matter
into the silent,
unforthcoming
hole in God's face

ORACLE WHEAT

> "Evolution and Diet: Bitter Consequences . . . wild plants
> . . . do not want to be consumed and thus make their
> opinion known by displaying all sorts of poisonous
> chemicals to discourage nibbling herbivores."
> —*THE ECONOMIST*, September 23rd, 2006

What ails me? The dead animals I eat or the 6 or 12,
multi-martyred grains of wheat, oats, barley
and their chaff? I am nipped in the throat
by the dissemination of this improved grass;
the still-husky, unmilled matter, whose
diminutive residues will allergize me into
my own elegy, if I don't keep my mouth shut.

My tender tissue has fallen under the thrall
of infusorians, the staves of these advanced grasses,
cereal aristocracies, who raise orb and sceptre
over our vast arable lands each summer.

Their aim is to turn us into them. They whisper of it
from breakfast to dusk, in speech that has the rasp
of yon other slithery oracle in the grass.
How they hiss and dismiss us
in their desiccated tongues

while the dry scales of their civilization stick
in my throat, condemning me to choke.
White whiskers and multi-gold eyes
peer past my thropple and pour down my gullet,
where barley, the hard-bald, buckshot of Helios
shoots. Under what Tsar have the stars mobilized
the steppes and valleys
into a peasant army of peas and pepper pods
against me?

I say to the wild vetch, be Irish, be wild pea, be
like me, or be a Quebecker,
                              say no to conscription,
do not enlist in this endless

subcutaneous skirmish!
I have no stomach for it either.

AN ILLUSTRATIVE LIFE

> "You don't need an equitable distribution (of wealth) to
> keep an economy humming."
> —Jared Bernstein, a liberal economist in Washington.

The scientist restricts his or her observations
to those resources, economically, essential
to keep the organism thriving.
My second cousin-by-marriage
crawled out of Canada with one kidney
and back to Bangor, Co. Down, Northern Ireland
where he joined the RUC, then CID.
He was the son of a gamekeeper on the Estate
of Lord Duffern & Ava—
with all the inside dope on resources
any poacher would love to have
He was an insider with an outsider's eye—
if you know what I mean.
In Canada (London, Ontario)
he was a fitter,
maestro of the workings in a sewing machine;
born tinkerer, he took such gadgets,
as he did poultry, apart
and put them back together,
a pheasant under glass
or a spindle in the needle drum.

He did well until an infection felled him,
but for no great duration—his wife worked
till he paid off the medical bills and they made it
back to the United Kingdom of National Health
for a fee-free final recovery.

Then again, my second cousin-by-marriage
was of the right height and intelligence

to pass the police exams and with a sixth sense
re foul play, past or potential, so strong
he was sent to CID, interviewing thieves
turned terrorist or vice versa,
making enemies of those
whose slippery and suspicious habits
he knew only to well.

He took early retirement and bought a pub,
which prospered, and a plane, which crashed
and he crawled out of—very upwardly mobile,
economically, but in permanent pain
with his back, which he preferred vodka to kill

until his operation. Then, he and his wife sprung
for a second pub, where the lordly,
Northern Irish horsy and working classes
were separated by a partition at the bar.
He removed the partition in an egalitarian gesture,
then put it back in when both sides
complained of the uncustomary exposure.

He throve, financially, until a stroke
took much of his memory
and he could barely remember
how well off or where he was. Still,
during that period when one sector of his mind
collapsed, my second cousin-by-marriage
did better and better with the small
percentage of him required
for things to go
great guns
and make a fiscal killing, but he kept saying
some peasant wanted a pheasant, and repeatedly
chuckled at this notion or tall order
for the day. His sons, who were born

into his publican's business, upped
the income and the outlets
and he throve some more, but could not
satisfy or supply that peasant
who haunted him
for a pheasant. He could remember
exactly where one was to be had,
but it was bad business for too little return.
         Would the peasant take
a drink of vodka
                     or poteen instead,
compliments of the house?

OUTDOING ARCHIMEDES

Article on the anniversary of the Greek victory at the sea battle
of Syracuse, which Archimedes is reputed to have secured by
setting fire to the enemy ships with a battery of mirrors.

How I'd like to mirror the sun,
     which slants over our roof
onto the larboard of the house,
     where it misses our deck
as that side, which ails greyly into winter, lit
     only by the colour of its own wood, a slow
glow of cedar quickening in the wet.

     I would like to arc mirrors into a bracelet,
the brilliant wrist, hand and fingers of which
     would touch our kitchen window
with the newly arrayed rays of the South.
     We cook and we eat, looking North—
feeling crushed into the blue bergs
     of the North Shore. The oranges
we pyramid in a bowl to squeeze or eat,
     their peels lie dumped in circles,
the dropped bloomers of the sun—
     Persephone's, where she dove
down to kiss the hot god of the South Seas.

We burn off the fleets of winter cloud
     using the wicks of dinner candles
twinkling in glasses of red wine with the 14% cheer
     of alcohol
from Down-Under in Australia;
     cheer, which like good sailors
or soldiers, we try to rekindle
     with the flint of a grin
into the steam on the bathroom mirror.

ON READING OF TWO PROGRAMS
CODE-NAMED *MINARET* AND *SHAMROCK*

Between 1967 and 1973, *Minaret* kept track of tele-
grams and phone calls in and out of the U. S.;
Shamrock, begun in 1947 for the censorship
of international telegrams, was shut down in 1975;
the Shamrock, code-named for the communications
Trinity: IT&T, Western Union and RCA Global

reported to the NSA 1 and thus St. Patrick's
teaching aid for making the mysterious obvious
was used for a paradoxical opposite: a two-in-one,
to expose, but keep privy to their intelligence
contacts between men, women and any alien
and dangerous order of the deity
or political idea.
            A more appropriate logo
could be cogged
from a 2 for 1 Pizza's: Panago's,
for example, but it would provoke an instant law suit
for misappropriation. Easier to rip off
a dead Celtic saint
or tower of Islam
in the days when religions where oblivious
to the taking of their sacred names, symbols
and places, commercially
in vain.
            My proposal is that never again
should the shamrock top a stack of dossiers
for scrutiny by any President, Prime Minister
or state's employee without fee.
            As to telegrams, telephone calls
and pirate-peeping at e-missives, a 1¢ tariff
for every second of listening-in,
or word read, same as for auteurs and artists
whose works are downloaded

as breezily
as flush toilets
with no water rates attached.
     A constitutional amendment to bring in
a Read and Listen Right
for Interesting-to-the-Government Anybodies
and their exchanges
of conscience or personal news and info.
     The commonweal has ageless precedent for it:
every soul pays a tithe for the services
of their God-booth in a church, mosque,
temple or synagogue, where one can monitor
and ponder the mysterious intent in the words
to and from the maker of disasters,
great hurricanes, tsunamis and the small
confusing kin of three-leaf clovers.

* (National Security Agency)

ON WHY THE SPORTS SECTION PASSES THE BALL, RELIGIOUSLY, TO THE BUSINESS PAGES IN THE DAILY PAPER

1. In the polo (water or horsy),
the jai alai (from Rio by the sea
to Trento below sea level
in the Dolomites), at racket,
hand, tennis, hurley,
cricket or at kiri tiki,
where the whole populace
of a Samoan village, to a man,
woman and child, takes part
with the long club-bat
to cleave or in turn
field and bowl the ball
across the common
where the road winds
around the wickets
at either end of the village
between the coconut-frond thatch
fales.
      Through the metamorphoses
of hard to soft, large to small,
ribbed to plain,
square-sectioned to stippled,
round to pointy-lugged oval,
the ball draws the masses
at all hours, weekdays,
Sundays and other feast,
fast and days of rest—to prayer
in the stands or in the locker rooms,
the select vestries of sweat, which must truly shoot
a divine migraine
through God's indivisible, yet equally-apportioned
support.

2. But what sort of supporter
is our God, whose coloured and numbered shirt
is of too many hues, prime and cardinal numbers
to bear looking at, or just the one colour,
saffron as the sun, those Buddha's boys don
to hum a mantra of infinite neutrality. Come to think
—who do Hare Krishnas root for? Or do they just dig
the one big round belly-ball of the god, Ganesh,
like the old bladder ball we used to boot
on a waste ground, amazed at the bounce and twang
the inflatable rubber inside gave the leather casing
when we punted it—the soar, almost solar,
launched from our instep, or paused
like the circle of the cosmos
under the soles of our feet, before
being passed
downfield.

Perhaps the god in the grass is that ball we follow,
which becomes the goal for those who hit it perfectly
at the right moment of play: the baseballer aiming for
the sky above the floodlights, the cricketer—an elm
behind the club house, where hats tilt
in the deck chairs with a nice drink
under the brims, levered up by a G & T as deftly
as the aluminium tab
on the soccer hoodlum's can of beer;
                                        its global message
gets relayed, like the palpable reply

to the monk-like prayer,
through the helmet and the head
of a player in a padded habit,
who passes it on
through the static-infested traffic
of pants and chants

in the football abbey
to a sure receiver, who drops to his knees
and thumps the sacred pigskin
on the appointed, painted place
after it has spun through air
into the incarnation of his hands
at its touchdown;
                    Jesus!

PLACE SETTING

*I dread Angela's eyes
on the Saturday "Style"
with update etiquette
section in THE GLOBE*

Cautioned, for eating like a garburator, and hence
ineligible for a place at fine tables
in England or Europe, he asks, "England
or Europe, where butter don't melt
in people's mouths,
so they can use their mouths as fridges,
right? "
           (The Thames with all those bridges
                       and gurgles under . . .)

He is not completely, but close to gross,
where he keeps himself,
                   (and his manners) teetering
over the edge, the steep foliage
of facial hair curled across the cliff of his lip
(hazards yawn or savoury morsels fall asleep there).

You ask him why does he do it? Well . . . because
the response he intuits from you makes him
the barbarian masticator at the plate,
and gives full play to his flavour-savers:
the lips and nostrils, the moustache.

           (Never the idle gob is he.)

But why did you, in your role as Chaucer's
Prioresse, who let no morsel from hir lippes falle,
put him
in rude and risible rumination
with you over every dish?

Among strangers he does discipline his chew
even in England or Europe,

But with you, it always provokes an argument
re: The Purpose of Good Manners—
to make others comfortable and for easy
intercourse? But unbreakable rules freeze all ease,
and the fingers
                    into the same china
                    as the cup

that slips and falls with a clatter and crash,
like comfort off the table.

If the real interest
lay in the food and the conversation of others, dear,

implements' rules of use
would be redundant at dinner.

But since he always perceives the primitive
in the polite, he says
                              in England or Europe,
the purpose of regulations with knife and fork
is
                    for the superior host and observer
                              to seize any miscue
as the moment to stick the cutlery ,
              not into the roast bœuf
or tidy Yorkshire pudding,
                              but the ruddy,
well cooked
              (in-his-own-embarrassment)
guest.

HIRUDO *NON* MEDICINALIS

Scientist at Work | Mark Siddall
His Subject: Highly Evolved and Exquisitely Thirsty
By CARL ZIMMER
Published *NYT*: February 7, 2006

On the rumps of hippopotamuses
there dwell large important leeches,
guzzle-cheeks, whose gizzards house
scads of merdacious bacteria as their base for protein,
an evolution of the worm some devil with diarrhoea
                                        has overseen.
This ruminant of blood and viruses—which patrols,
rearguard, in an apocalypse of mud holes—
suits a vision from Hieronimus
Bosch, while its host wades up in leather breeches,
like something out of Nostradamus.

We marvel at how vile our needs are;
functions whose names we dare not utter nor do
                                        without,
whose specimens scientists are apt to collect in a jar—
if suitably outlandish. Although this leech is not
                                        medicinal,
won't forsake the haunch of its host for you,
be applied as anti-coagulant
to any private part of you or as gross simulant
of love as we believed girls' glands would be to our
wee boys', yet, as though they were rainbow trout,
we fished for them in the Meadow with our bare toes.
                                        Slainte var!

Said Billy Myers, 'if I couldn't tolerate a leech t'latch
onto me, no girl'd ever do me, I'd never let'er fingers
                                        drain
my brain while she twiddled my gadget and gave my

                                    balls a scratch.
I'd be done out o' the kiss o' two female gubs,
the one in her bod' an' th'on' in her head that'd suck
the thatch off my stupid tongue.' I don't know why
                        Billy had such truck
with these sexual antipodes and their lovely,
            ugly infirmities. Seeing his Da's face
gulder, "Bloodsucker," and quiver at the lips of Billy's
                  gorgeous mother, Grace—
Mr. Myers with his skin-full of alcohol greeting
                  his salubrious match?
Her—drain that beer-bum, or get her money back
                  on the contain . . .
er—fat chance! She was above that hippo rear-end
      sipping klatch!

FROM ANY PAPER, ANY MAG, ANY DAY

What would be your weapon of choice
To bring down the house—an ICBM
Or Looney Tune?

Islam, Christianity, Jewry
are God's Three Stooges,
the Curly, Larry and Moe
of the mountain-desert-
and-oasis set, who never
get it together for the
singular divinity.
They have knuckleheaded ideas
and directions. They crack skulls.
They hear each other wrong,
can't "sympathize" their watches
on a timetable to eternity.
They tweak and pull each other's ears,
heads, and other body parts to see
if their associate will learn and remember
whatever their loud gabbledy squabble
erased from hearing. Curly
and Larry never fail
to appear startled; Moe bubbles,
his ire boils on the burner
of a prodigious disgust
under his bowl cut,
his medieval tonsure.
They ask the One what they ought to do
to remedy this slapstick comedy
and cannot hear the One for everyone
in the audience
screaming, "Do what you do best.
Clown, don't kill. Put on skits
and sketches. Skits and sketches!

Perfect the indignity
of the pratfall.
Today, let a new law of reciprocity
be laid upon the land
and pasted to the lampposts: a skit for a skit,
cartoon for cartoon, a caricature
for a caricature of the most silly.
Let the peoples take to their drawing,
not their launching pads.

And you know silly is what it has always meant.
Silly: you *blessed* idiots.

ANOTHER DEATH OF THE DAILY PAPER

The image of the woman or the man bunkered
In a chair behind stacks of his or her favourite
Daily paper—the weekend sections set aside,
To be hunkered over in a separate section
Of the suite, the bathroom, or kitchen nook—
Has always prevented you from subscribing,
Until, having time and intending to be wise
On your retirement, you take one out, pledging
never to lapse in your religious reading.
But absorption in juicy articles, a discussion,
A bark from the street, or your spouse's halted
Progress on transplanting an old rhodo
Brings you outside, where the light
Still stands tall and there to greet you
Like its altered pal and it makes you
Over-emulate the small, squinting sage
Behind whose hooded lids,
The eyeballs squirm with embarrassment.
You see in black and white and the new
true life daily is hugely coloured.
When you go back into the hall,
It has filled with what has just been sent
And taken in your door, ready or no.
Laggard or plain dullard
You fall behind the calendar in your reading,
And the math of the compound omission
Gets you: three days in arrears by week fifteen,
Four by week sixteen, five by seventeen
Until the walls are smudged, and the floors
And tables, covered in a grey-black swath
Of newsprint, then tidied pillars of crushed
Columns with compressed, but pristine
Columnists, still dying to be read. Your daughter
Arrives from some South Sea island

Where she has been living with her surfer husband.
She hugs your shuddering spouse, and for Christmas
Cancels the subscription,
            Then kicks your lazy lector's ass.

3. CONVICTION

The oldest love poem is found in Turkey,
Inanna's to Dumuzi,
The priestess of love and fertility,
The shepherd god's all-hallowed floozy,
Who made love for the sake of the lamb
On the mountain and corn on the plain.
Written in Sumerian, in stone iambs,
No doubt, but somewhere in Spain
Outpost of the Moor, I felt it half true
For I inherited the flesh of it, new from you.

CONCUPISCENCE

Mornings, after the owls' oratorio in the beach wood,
the ditch and its cat-tail cornucopia would

swipe
with its wicked tiger-green stripe

and attack
our ankles, where we kissed over the smell of black

water running from the sinks and tubs into the grass
before filters were put in or drains laid. Alas,

the inedible flowers, weeds had a magnificence
and the pollution of our embrace, incense

of egg and onion breath added our shocking inventory
to corrupted sea and earth. On the promontory

of your breast and under an itchy blanket
I played my glad part in it.

That bit of land was always deadly damp and flat,
there used to be a farm there

In asthma hollow, from Jericho to Kitsilano
The mist and fog flow

In among the condos
Where, like grey dough,

They clog my eyes, nose and throat as though
For a moment the sorrow

Of Chief Kitsilano seeped into
The lining and leaky walls, new-

Bred by a rash
Of building code as virulent as the night-green Irish

Yew's.
It was not the city cops or their truncheons that slew

You, nor the malignant horns or bray
Off the bay—

The preservatives for property in the dark yew hedges
Nor even the hedge funds, but the blockage

Along 16th Avenue, where a farm
Squatted over a bog before you came and the harm

Settled into a daily drizzle
with the news that *Kitsilano is ill.*

ORAL ARCHITECTURE (1) *ALLIUM CEPA*

In the sky, over the bald plain, the farmers plant the image of what they grow in the ground: a dome, shaped like the gilded skin of an onion with all its complicated accretions, glaze, and crystalline concentrations inside. I am a passer-through, an un-enduring, unreliable observer. But to my flawed perception, Ukrainians of old, Russian-Russians, Belarusians and Saskatchewaners share a uniform interest in the onion dome—that architectural tuber.

When over the wilderness of wheat, eyes fasten on its glowing gold, it can make them weep, involuntarily. Curving around inside—from weddings, funerals, and plain ordinary services—the transparent and endless sound of hymn and prayer foliate; parishioners enter, with the loud wind in their ears, the sun's trumpet gleam in their eyes which still sounds the all-clear after the thunderstorm flattened the wheat before them all the way to church.

They come in with memories and feelings so tightly ringed, one upon the other, their minds and chests so constricted with the inexpressible that they cannot speak. They come to lay out their small collections, the sheaf and the pumpkin, the bail at harvest time to redeem the pain of the field. They wet their lips, reluctant to say goodbye and abandon the few words of faith that orb them with their fellow worshippers, the feed and tack man, the waggoner or stranger like me who rolls in on his way to the coast, looking for a berth to take him back the way he came.

On the beach, dark brown globes at the end of bull kelp remind me of them later. I pick them up out of the sea and look into their deep unreflecting glaze and think upon these viscous domes, floated in off the ocean plain, uprooted by storms as far away as Polynesia and

Eurasia, vessels that ride it out on waves, the orisons of the ocean which boom over its bulbed walks, the kelp-cobbled vestibules with mile-long sashes, underwater.

Sea beetroot, embedded red-brown eyes, ear plugs torn from the tidal roar so I hear and see again the Byzantine skin, the crackling packet of tearful prayer, the golden crepitations of an onion in the resounding sun of a Pacific *Pater Noster*, our Father Who Art in Heaven.

ESTEVAN

for Eli Mandel

The hanger clangs,
thin drone of bells
in the wooden hive
of the wardrobe.

I am going out in this
dressed for a drenching,
looking up at the sky
for something I forgot

to reach for, to wear,
that is always overhead.

The sun, like my skull cap,
my yarmulke. A low prayer
on the horizon

and crooked
white wire hanger
of lightning

that God, laying bare
a broad shoulder of cloud, unbent
from under the robe of rain
in his big room, and straightened

to hoke at a stubbled bung
of clay and unclog
a trillion feet
of prairie.

to grow wheat on.

HARD-BOILED, PORT ALBERNI, 1966

In a jar, on the bar, in an aqueous tabernacle,
the eggs—misshapen billiard balls or eye-whites
of blind Cyclops—bulge. These glazed delights
are bald pates; shaven images (graven by the oracle

hens) of human crania. The clear solution comes not
from some wizard to preserve them, but a vein of vinegar,
that might well have spilled from the wrists of sailors
  who are
sprinkled in brine so often on the Alberni Canal, they rot

down to these old farts at the tables that marinate in
  shadow
under the crystal ramparts of the salt
cellars. Hunger keel-hauls our boozers' fingers to a halt
at our lips, ere the bassoons of the saloon blow

the portside doldrums out—we kiss these albino ovals
  that consort
in our belly like bosom buddies as blue as *mon vieux*
  Roquefort.

GULF ISLAND

A snowflake is a cold cobweb
that catches spiders and other insects
unawares, reduces them—if we're lucky, to zero. Sects
of all sorts pray for clemency and an ebb
in the winter weather, but minus the swarms of summer
  mosquitoes
as a consequence. Oh Lord, give us balanced blessing.
Yet its scales,
like silks and sicknesses, are made of the disparities:
  whales
go blind in Hecate Strait from the overflow
of the septic tank for our cabin with a view;
fire and flood still calibrate the wild West's
actuarials, and our helicopters are too old for sea
  rescue.
The lowly lake noses back into the living room, to
  reinvest
in lost habitat, and its water laps at my armchair,
like a dog. Give it a bone, you say, you know it's only
  fair.

THE LETTING DOWN

It cannot come on full,
your pleasure,
like a light, or the one tulip
in a room
with all the power
of the electrical grid
and garden behind it

working full out;

it must pass
through a subtle lampshade
and late afternoon
of a despair,
          the staid
and stolid
      reading reading
into the dark corners
with the discreet, yet stark
beauty of their details:

a steel hairpin, whose serrated side
mimics a riff of silver water
seen from the air;

a bird in the corner window,
caught between the skyb'rd
and the sideboard's
          vase
below;

     the hair,
  held up in
honour of your head, so hale and prolonged—

like an auburn grenade
                    I cannot let you toss
because it pains
                    and my life is dimmed
when you push back in the pin.

LITTLE LILITH IN THE HALL

Light splashes off a crystal door handle
onto a grandchild's saffron sandal.

When you open your palm and let the handle go,.
the sandal makes you think, though you do not know

immediately, of a mulled yellow for the hall,
a paint to make you at ease, numbed even, null

yellow as Pernod and water,
to mix and match, later,

with sunlight's natural
buttercup, not the horrid yellow reveille of the daffodil

night and morning. A kindly serpent yellow
that will induce in you a low bellow

at the familiar slime under the sandal,
and instead of flying off the handle

—lay you down to lie
on your belly. You need laid down to lie,

silly as it may seem, to learn your head
is filthy but innocent as muck, at home in bed

under the cowl of the skunk cabbage glow,
the stink and sting of its cobra yellow.

WE LET THE BACK DOOR SWING

As if it were still on the pneumatic hinge
we took off a year ago,
as if one touch will let us
swing back together and close
like a door into its jamb
for the night.

As it is, the words
flanged to our throats
join the bang.
We blame each other
for removing the pneumatic.
We make love, but the more
we pass through this screen door
of summers, the louder
and harder, the unautomatic
bang of that blessed door.

ON THE LOWER FRASER, LULU ISLAND
AND RICHMOND

Our souls meander like rivers through us
in old age, past Surrey and Richmond, old-country
    names
for the rich world taken from the indigene, whose
    claim is
not a plough, but a paddle to till the rich acres of
    liquid. It's still precipitous
hydrology, this Fraser, which, in its young phase,
    plunges
through the soft places in the rock and eventually
totes everything—like one of nature's grunges,
all the minerals it mines and logs it lops—down into
    the valley,
where sturgeon settle with a city of eggs glistening in
    their belly
deep beneath our consciousness. At Langley,
    passengers from these parts
step onto a steel sandal to cross it and pay the ferryman
or never get out of the car. The road just stops and
    starts
over, where quick as glances, the fish swim past and
    push on
into the swollen clay-grey eye of the Fraser that stares
    back at itself from the ocean.

FROM THE NET BEHIND THE BOAT

Experience is an old cart that comes by every day
with fish to sell;
we are attracted to it, but at the same time
cannot bear the smell
which is far too raw; once it is well-cooked,
we learn to enjoy the taste and to be able
to digest it.

Turning it into cuisine
and ingesting in this second course
is named knowledge, and if we want
to drive the cart before the horse,
we need great clairvoyance
or a readymade hindsight to hold the reins
and back up into the odour, into the harbour,
and out toward the seines
in the ocean the fish come from.

That way the horse can slip
and the cart fall in;
it can be so spectacular,
we prefer it.

YELLOW ISLE

He used his old pulp mill boots
Instead of flower pots.

At the Court of Incorrections
the indictments add up on an abacus
of bristle pine cones,
        small as noses,
that sneeze a coat of yellow pollen
onto the sidewalk, as you step around it,
like nature's jaundiced
        judgement on you.

Asters and late sunflowers?
        You should get sick,
not at what was done wrong, but what
didn't get done. Stepping, slipping
        through the sudden fall
and dying years of friends
        into a bottle—the perfect djinn
of omissions. You still can't believe pollen
        so late in the year
or that disease understands no season
nor compelling reason.
        You did not jay walk
across the yellow island
on your stroll, but through its Petty Sessions
the Court of Incorrections pursues you
with the wheeze and whistle
of your own asthma. Policeman of the graveyards,
who could only see the undertaker's flowers growing
in his boots at Jack Ashbridge's front door.

Everything has its beard
Of yuletide frost,
And the gate,
Its set
Of fingerprints
To tell what I've
Been through.
That flash of bird
Wing in bare light—
A new remindering
Of eyelids'
First opening—settles
Like sight:
A flurry, then a conviction
That what is there is there,
As balanced as the board
I nailed straight on the fence
With the aid
Of a spirit level, to be
An endless impromptu

Landing strip
For sparrows

RACCOON, SKUNK, SQUIRREL & CAT

The racoons come to take up bulbs
or worms from the lawn and raised beds,

or the challenge to out-garden my wife;

for they belong in her bandit league
of poke and pillage lawn husbandry.

How often has she dug out its grass
in favour of a fruit or flower

while the drain lid by the basement door,
an iron honeycomb a-hive with grubs,

is plucked up and sacked
surreptitiously by the skunk,

who keeps to the walls
and noses the downspouts
at the four corners of the house

like a building inspector
suspicious of the structure's overall stability
and power to grow

                (houses do grow,
but only with the blows
of a carpenter's hammer)

but the place does get a reluctant pass and blessing
from the property-priest in black and white scapular.

Rats—
        slip or wobble by
along the telegraph wires
like gobbets of semen
in a furry handkerchief,
or the dirty phone calls—
                        my wife
abhors.

Their related vermin,
squirrels from back East,
undulate blackly or greyly
over the same lines,
like the curves along the chart
of my wife's stock portfolio,

which takes her into a great lift
or depression
daily.

The cat who craps
in the parsley,

        the grey acorn-planting
        gardener squirrel—

for such she keeps a water cannon
or a bucket handy.

The cat will shake and sulk off,
dampened and offended,

but always when she squirts the squirrel,
and hits with her distaste,

it retreats (far from her liking)
to lick the wet blitzkrieg

off its creepy-crawly
cairn,

      its furry drumlin
with surprised
and surprising relish.

You come up to the soul
after this long time away
and say, "How you doin?"
like Tony Soprano, "Ain't bin
mopin, I hope?"

And like an old girl friend
you left in bed
or on the dance floor
a long time ago, she turns
and says, "Do I know you?"
and you say, "Youse do.
I just doan come here so often
as I use to, capish? Jeeze,
what you want me to do—
beg, break both my legs,
do in my chest, crack
my skull, have a heart attack,
then come back to see you?"

And the soul looks down on
your come-on,
"No attacks, no cracks,
no breaks—you have to come
to me like you are going
to live in that body you have,
forever. After how
yous've treated it,
how will youse treat me?"

REMEMBERING LONDON

As soon as you land, out of the heavens
as it were, in 1990, you still see London in 1957.
You think if you say it louder the point
will be evident; broader perspectives will anoint
my mind like oil, but you can't interest
me in this bungee jump of nostalgia, which best
expands off bridges, and high places,
castle keeps, even Selfridges. For you two paces
on Seven Sisters cross Camden Town, if constancy
to your 7 league memory is kept. The necromancy
of one step up to your rain and sun-scrubbed face
blots out backdrops for me, even under the auspice
of St. Paul's. You are the one thing
that recalls all this city magnified in our meeting.

DIARY OF A MAD HOME DECORATOR

Through the window falls the thin
grey shadow of day under the inside sill,
which I could be here painting till
I die, to brighten.

I   THE CASE FOR THE CRAVEN

Penny Keith says shyness is egotism out of its depth,
Some say the cunning of curiosity is an animal
born of shyness seeking camouflage
in every quirk of colour and foliage,
where twigs are stitches for a dress that renders
appearance minimal.

II   THE SERPENT CLASS

I wore clothes,
cravenly, unceremoniously,
like a snake in the ends of its old skin
I looked for a pit to crawl into. Or a cove,
my Carnalea   *Car-nah-lee—*
might be Irish for the *cairn* and for the *poem,*
> how one might lie, syllable for syllable
> upon the other, in a great lay and lament,
> not *Carnally* (as a man on a woman
> groaning in an erotic grotto
> through a duet of grunted lyrics.)
Or perhaps it was for this I was squirming
behind my foreskin, then and now, the seminal
head of the sea-seeking serpent, shaped
like a harpoon, and drawn to where the odour was
wild and wide
> to don a cloak of air on the rocks
> where I sloughed off my traces,
where your ocean came in, fierce and erasive,
and I flinched, like a snail, at your splash of salt
on my back.

AUBADE

The sun rises at four now,
and I am not up out of bed to greet it,
my mind is already a small buzzing dome of day,
full of bees like good Muslims,
hymning to Mecca;
but like a lighthouse with a Cyclops eye,
it turns and turns—the beacon in my brain,
made of light all night
looking for the relief of day
to take over the vigil
for everything alive about me.

AIRS, STRONG TO GALE FORCE

Would you want to be a bird in a wind like this?
Like a harvester's slats at high green wheat
Branches thrash its kernel of song, the tweet.
Lovers of air fall out of it; paralysis

Takes down appliances in the mod-con house;
The thing inside them, sorely smitten; our faith
And roast dinner expectation, an odorous wraith;
In place, we hear the skitter of our heart mouse.

While wind flies and screeches in mangled choirs,
Warbles and gobbles like all birds and prey at once—
Its quavers of music sparked by a tree, this dunce
Fails to read overhead, off a staff of power wires,
Flashing beak(ons), eagle, falcon, hawk's, announce
The wild tit and turkey ire a jealous breeze acquired.

HOW HURTFUL?

When two are talking, in one corner of the room,
always, there are two whispering, in another
wondering what they say.

A butterfly descends on the parsley plant.
How fussy and green must those crenulated prickles be
to its feelers and its feet?
As scratchy as when eaten raw the parsley cleats
onto the soft tissue of my throat. Nectar too pungent
to be aught but vegetable TSP,
a stiff cloak of aggressive chlorophyll!
Is this what the quixotic butterfly mistakes
on the harsh parsley: the hard dolour?
What I feel for on the bold, curious colour
of your red fingernails? A coercive thrill,
harder than hell, whose anticipation rakes

my soft spots like grandkids spying the dots
of Cadbury's Smarties their eyes gorge on. Oh
you pepper the torpid pit of my stomach
and jolt me from my decrepit rage,
raised bed of eight foot ties and black pots
of herbs from Home Depot,

a puppet stuttering on a five-finger alpha-
bet into the alveoli of a labyrinthine girl.
Perhaps the butterfly lands
on the wisdom of these painful pollens
or the comb scratches no more than when Alfalfa
makes a tilt for Darla with a curl.

I AM EMBARRASSED TO SAY
I CAN'T PUT A NAME TO IT

Less leaves, more birds
To look at.
Beaks and tails tilt earthwards
Like little oil rigs
Or the pump
On an artesian well,
Or camel hump's
Dip and lift in the desert
Near the Nile. Water and wings
In the nowhere, installed.
These black-capped and tan-wing ones, ahem!—
What are they called,
Now I can see them?

EMPERICLES

1. Do you aver it because it is real
and substantial, a product of age
and wisdom—or recognize it
as yet another wrinkle among the many
accumulated on the face
in the process of growing old.

2. A bird sat
on a branch up high
and said love me,
but how could I
with a wee elusive chickadee
or tiny tomtit like that?
Easier to swat
the hummingbird, noseeum, or the fly
in the murky corner of your eye
that skids off a mouth at
the rate of a missed kiss in the tea-
brown evening. How accurate,
unerring, a lover's lips must be
to land on that small plea and cure it.

CONVICTION

Like the feet of children tingle
And smart on the shingle,
Whose faces glow and sting
With sun and seaside visiting,

As spiders as green as can be,
On evenings as wide as the sea,
Walk, without the slightest fuss,
In harmony with the octopus

On legs as fine and fair
As baby hair,
Or platinum eyelash
Of the moon, whose light will wash

Over—as though the car were coral,
A reef of metal
In the night. Like they breed dilemma
On the radio antenna,

Webbed through the air, the sweet
Music of their feet
Treads into my head
The stickiness of love I dread.

Like them I walk a plank
Of moonlight for my lank
Captaincy of love—old stiff
Transported in a skiff,

Whose oars are fourfingers,
And hull, a hand
That seeks your face, as if it were Van
Dieman's Land

4. MY SIDE

A question of some import for me
from Nor'n Ire-land (emphasis on the ire)
conveyed by a person
of some influence and literary persuasion,

"Wouldn't you like to be seen
On our side of the tradition?"

"No, not really," says I. "I like my
Neither-Norness."

INSIDE

There is a mangle in my chest
that makes the constant cranking
of my respiration somewhat antique,
an ancient pressing process
of arm and handle, dark, wrought-iron
hubs and water-weathered
wooden rollers.

Sud-sped and expelled.
the breath passes in long coarse sheets
laundered down to the raw cloth,
folded in two or three to fit the gap
in the dripping lips of the rollers,
but they twist; they misalign and stick,
and the handle has to be turned in reverse—
the breath squeezed out. Out, not in.
And every time one is done,
the work hangs perfectly unseeable—
or unseemly in the air
with some grievous stain or sputum
stuck to it like the gobs
off the glue-coloured washing soap,
or the olive green bricks that tempt one
to hurl them at whoever ordered
the heavy work, the heaving up and down
in the tub of my chest.

I ask whose laundry this is.

Clouds fly by, unafraid to be on show
in this warm day outdoors,
where the long grass
is about its business of podding
and popping, the whin—what they call

broom here—compelling me to say
it is time to spring clean from the inside out,
and in the big demesne of the atmosphere,
one stands lost in a corner of one's yard—
energized and lost, panting
wanting to know—whose laundry
this is I do inside me.

BAD

So near and narrow-minded are my kind
that we hold a razor blade
of suspicion and rage
   wedged permanently
   in our heads
which cuts our selves
in two—into the Irish
and the not-Irish; it gives
our eyes a gleam stronger
than the steel grey
and planished blade
of the Irish Sea and sky,
   edged
by the low rolling breakers
of the Lough
   and whetted
regular on the long brown strap
of the Lagan.
For as long as I remember
I have tried to love these two
parts of me, but am
as unable as anyone,
   holding
   hot chestnuts
   or spuds
   spiked
   with Wilkinson sword edges
   in his hands,
to juggle
his own nativity.

MY SEA SIDE

The Far South I first saw
      from dunes
that bevel a wide shallow pan
      of a bay
at Clonakilty
      Through a serial glaze
of cream-capped breakers
      rolling
off a scoop of light
      on the horizon

      which held the Azores
and more Atlantic
      roaring
down the narrow channel of my vision
      from the Cape

like the water columned
      through the hollow panhandle of sand
to sear
      under an August sun
the burner on the bay
      behind

      That is how I first felt
the warm flow of afar
      in that outflow
after making appliqué
      of my pink body
to the freeze and frieze
      of surf
plastered to the shore

then through that narrow conduit
      plunging
into the simmered river
      of the southern ocean
in my mind.

      Never in this world
did I think I would go wide
      to go long or that I would bungle
the longitudes and latitudes
      in the grid talk
of North American football,

      or learn
the buoys and barrens of the Gulf
      the abstract venture of its imagination
on the other side of the ocean
from one   José Emilio Pacheco
by
      going back to sea
with him

    A shadow
    from the steep sea escarpments
    or the undulating stain
    of a fish, or bird or stone.
    Nothing stirs under the sun
     as if the sea
    is the stopped heart of all motion.
    Ever since water became sea
    and lost the planet
    with these same waves it has been appealing
    in a keening, wet-eyed orison
    that switches octaves suddenly to rage,

storm of the tormented.
This reach of wide water
to me is the whole ocean
or as if it were
because always I come back to look at it.
And when I think of sea
this image forms.
I carry it so deep inside
that its murmur
I tell you
is like a property of my blood.
And when I am no longer here
to look at and to love it
the sea will have dried out into desert
—to this, the vantage of my brittle subjectivity—
scattered with the spray
when my grey ashes light up for one moment
and I am once more
an atom in the nothing or the life everlasting
in the total sea of that undivided ocean

The ashes I have
        lie in a rusted bucket
in our garden.
        The rain pours off the good roof
of the doghouse
        where I put the powdery pail
from the fire.

        I lay them in the lane,
pale grey sky, pale grey winter ashes.
        This week or next.
to Mexico or Sooke—
        seasides

always seasides—
        to water grey and flat as a dead grate
or blue as a blaze of coke
        tinkling across the surface
of a watchman's
        brazier

        Mood moves faster than I do
sails to sea
        where my dust
is a drift of plankton
        the stream of fodder
mites love on land
        not yet
my widow's
        for the mantle

        I swim daily
in myself, I dream
        nightly
of the sea that isn't me
        that grows luminous
north or south
        with the phosphorescence
of what I feel
        and dream
Let it lead me,
        loop me, be
the tentacular
        liquid teacher
of my life
        Let it not become
the panhandle
        of sand
for where I cook
        my sad

crash-landed
      Canada
goose

      Or dry clean
in the chemical heat
      the evaporating
ash of dowdy, daily
      despair.

I am 66 years old—
      Route 66
through the viscera
      of the sea
edgy, aging,
      always changing
in the current of its moods

The New York Times' 'Quebec Journal' by Clifford Krauss, Tuesday, October 25, 2005, quoting Lise Payette from *Le Journal de Montreal*: "We Quebecers fancy our heroes a little bit cheeky, defeatist, hesitant, unsure of themselves, alcoholic, a little or even a lot unreliable, a little bit fraudulent or even a little drugged," she explained. "We like to say they are like us. "

We come from flaky, flawed folk, villains
who hang onto the neck of what they have,
like a wife-beater to his love,
before she betrays him with a handsome
black haired, blue-eyed Roman Catholic man,
who lacks the squint to sicken her

or worse still, the wife falls for her ladyship,
the Virgin Mary.

We prefer our women to defend the kitchen
against filchers, skivers and ginger Toms
and give in to our exclusive whims and whimpers

when we are tipsy with alternatives
to the usual. A Molotov cocktail

or two, shared
with the Papists.

GUYS *ET GARS*

Phrases sizzle around the tribe
like fat in a fryer
for the frites
through Acapulco. The *ah-oui?*
promenade past these signs made for them
in hot heaven,
              like *my* own tribe—the *oh-aye?*
who apply that expression, constantly,
their sceptic sauce to any piece of gossip,
or good one offered them to sample
and swallow from someone else's mouth;
              and from my new tribe,
              their cue of non-cognition—the *eh.*

The *eh*
and the *ah-oui*
talking the bulk of the way up a seaside hill,
where steps to the side of the broad sidewalk fall
like cliffs onto platformed panorama of gingham tables
and gigantic enticers in the restaurants and bars.
In this same instant, on the other side of an ocean
and a sea, as at large and as loud, my nieces and nephews,
the great and the great-great, my cousins and company
are out on the tiles and sand of the simulated
blue green sea, a promenade in Torremolinos.
              In the air their noses scribble odes
to the odour of chips; they trail the *craic* with them
through the midway of the retail esplanade
and buffet the shops' show windows with guffaws,
their whole clatter of chatter and grinding,
shattered glass accent of an earthquake.
When inspiration weakens,
everything is just *brilliant,*
their one adjective *uber alles.*

Meanwhile, it's cool for the *eh* and *jolie,*
for the *ah-oui,* jolly as their ancestors, going to fish
for land with a musket over the shoulder;
our guys, the loyalists, got the frigid tits of a continent
and the north of a wind-riddled island
for their troubles; for which they hoot
like disbelievers, *eh, oh aye?*
the *gars,* still the carousers and *coureurs,* continue
the campaign for their place of licence in the sun, talk
through noses squeezed against the moving window
of an Acapulco car-rental
or revolving restaurant. But all did gain
this distinction, a sound Mexicans and Spaniards
could tell them by a mile or kilometre away,
                    the *oh-aye,* the *eh* and the *ah-oui,*

like the squeaky tires of an SUV, the unabashed
out to have a bash at their favourite hash
on holiday.
            It gives me a buzz, it calls me to them
like a fly to a drain, how they refuse the napkin
for the gravy of their indiscretion
streaming from the lip

while seasoned with marijuana, Domecq or tequila
shooters,

they vie from first thing in the morning
to bake or French fry—
those *ah-oui, eh, oh-aye*—
like the promised *frites,* the chips
off old potatoes

in the sun.

145

WHAT IS THE FIRST THING YOU DO
IN THE MORNING?

My mother used to throw water on her face,
first thing; my Da lit a whole cigarette
or a butt he plucked, like the stained stem
of a mushroom, from his waistcoat pocket
by the bed—depending
on that day of the week's distance
from payday.

The first thing that brings one
to consciousness in the morning—
what's yours?

What action repeats,
like a common crow
or half-decent song bird?

Is it the black ritual
of coffee or rain
in the gutter of winter,
sun in the summer window?

If you were to sweeten your life,
starting first thing in the morning,
which would you choose—
prayer or pastry?

DRESSED TO KILL

(A Love Story)

His uniform was a cloth cap, a scarf
over a stud and hard-collarless neck.
He read cowboy books at 120 pages
or 28,800 words an hour, waiting
for a glimpse of her who couldn't
read a word, but who had this ultimatum
written all over her: love me, love the Union—
not the small u of man and woman, but the big U
to King Billy and all that *that* Willy stood for.

      When her beau went
to sign his name in blood
on the Covenant, not to be bettered
by him, he did too and inked his own life
onto the line to fight the English in order that Ireland,
and if not Ireland, Ulster
might remain part of a United Kingdom.
      Thus did he learn fine terms
and to talk
      in the clauses of causes

      He quit the low windowsill
at the foot of Israel Street, but sat and read
on the ships and the trains till he debarked in France,
      in the over-there
with the Ulster Volunteers, now the Royal
Ulster Rifles, as a Lewis gunner
his sights set for him now
      'to kill Gerry—with whom,'
as he said, he had no quarrel!

All for a union
with a little four-foot-eleven Ulsterwoman,
        who to him was
        the same size as
        the province her first beau
died for, leaving her
a handsome son of Ulster behind.

He had no quarrel
with that either, having to bear
the weight of the handsome dead man
as well as his son on his shoulder
        —like some circus
St. Christopher in a tableau—
        he saw himself going around
        and around the ring,
as much a mockery as Wild Bill Hickock
with Lord Edward Carson cracking the whip
        with every flip
        of the page in his Shankill-Road-cowboy
        book.

He never properly reconciled
to his loyalty, the sorry success
of killing those with whom he
had no quarrel
        to win what he wanted
        from those with whom he did.

One of the first times I met him
in his penthouse on Calle Lerma,
his French wife, Marie-Jo, came in with a
new make of cookie she had just bought him.
He offered me one of her discoveries.

Octavio Paz, the son, the point of your pen
incising the word dark and luminous as the memory
of Paz, the father, the ends of his moustache
dunked in dark wine, blacked out—
like match ends pitching toward the ground—
the incendiary afternoons go out, farther South
down Puebla-way. You see him
on another return from the States
with cash for the cause. The division rises within you
for the hero and the tippler; Zapata and his Division,
that cause provided for
a little further.

His horse expels a thin shell of breath—
which way the agent, the man,
which way for your words
opening all doors in the dark evening

What are you waiting for? asks your mother
as he dodders onto the veranda, as the breath
of the horse, History, breathes backward
and away,
extracting, expatriating
the soul through the ornamental spaces
in the trellis.

How much will either of you alter,
in spite of the iron will behind the words,
in spite of the Santo Tomas,
thick with its own season of sun,

and the mescal, porous and hard
as the stones that cleave

Mitla to its hill, or your tongue,
Octavio, that never drank a drop of it,

to the roof of your mouth when I ask,
"Is there any duty free
I can bring you from the North,
next time?"

DINNER WITH A LATE COMMUNIST FRIEND

1

When Indarki was in bed with typhoid
in Mexico City, his father, Ramón,
was disappeared from under our noses,
like a dinner taken away from the table,
our daily bread which came with blessings
and discussions not of God,

but the Party, PTR—
(Partido de Trabajadores Revolucionario,
the Worker's Revolutionary Party),

which Ana, his wife, Esperanza, his mother,
and the brothers, Fernando and Manuel,
two of the six present and one sister, Mara,
sons, Iker and Indarki and we
sat through, like glazed goodies for dessert.

We did not think how to see the hands
on the clock, glued like honey to the hour,
or the moment of our dispute
instilled
            in the amber of those evenings
like a golden fossil,

oh, the clearness of the difference now.

We just sat on, like the jellied fruit—the yams,
bristling in corn starch, bought from a bucket
off an Indian woman who goes by howling,
"*Camote.*" The yams sunk,

like the darkened body parts of Quetzalcoatl,
our evening star, in a silvery swirl of syrup
and galvanize.

      One of Ramón's causes
she happens by, regularly, to do her daily vending
and to confer in passing on the latest representation
in her dispute with her brother

who would cut her off like a bad half hectare
from a rich sale of family land.

                        Caustic
about his causes and on couches
and lazier than the stuffed chiles lying
on the sides on the plate, the conversation
lolls; we long for him
to turn up with his bite,

                    the leftovers,
of his mayoralty campaign,
like grape skins turning to rancid
wine in his mouth

through a second fermentation,
the aftertaste teaching something special.
not there in the first flavour:

rumination.
          . And now we mull
it, too: the cud, then
thud of his absent body.

2.

Usually, when I wash them,
bake peppers right—
as I cook them, they become
vegetable squid, rubbery-brittle,
a queer candy polyp
flavoured with sweet water
and earth, like his body must be,
sliced into eight or nine pieces
in a sack
somewhere, soaking in a well,

hung there in parts unknown
by two *federales*
to cure *el cabrón*—the sick, dirty
goat, who goaded them to slaughter
over their dislike, while we peer
with his mother, six brothers,
sister and his sons over the tables
into the evenings and listen
for the clunk of a bucket from the well
expecting him to be dished up,
the choicest pieces of goat

still ready to butt us
in the belly and the soul,
with the latest line
to his dismembered

dream recipe
for revolution.

As I went to our gate,
a knot of wood fell out of a board
at my feet

like an eye out of a head,
an Indian eye.
or older yet,
the forefolk's who see
us as leaves
off their tree,
in one long autumn.

The hardest wood is kept
For the hardest look.

Our children put their live eyeballs
to the empty socket,
and its shallow shell and shadow
turns theirs as dark as a knot.

They see everything in the lane,
passing. The severe
sooty blue
in the floppy, red socket
of the poppy glares
an agreement.

Unreal!

Each, in order,
the eyes of my children turn
like a key
in the gate
and they look back
into the garden
at the knot
in my hand
as if I am holding
the transience they have
seen in its place.

CHOCOLOPA

The children chase chocolopa,
a pellucid flea or shrimp that skips
and sinks into the grains of sand
as totally as a drop of water—
                                    something spat
                                    into life,
                                    out of the perfect blue sky
                                    by the perfect blue sea.

Thirteen days of precipitation,
we live north of this moment
in Audencia.

We think of exchanging
rain for snow
                        or chocolopas.

Rain, the rheum
of heaven blesses
when expelled;
                                    spit
                                    in the hand,
                                    the seal of faith
                                    on the deal; *It's spitting,*
they say of the rain
sealing the contract
on contact with the earth
for the fall—the sky's
to the ground. As if the two agree:

I wash your back of sand, loam or clay—
red, yellow, white or grey—
if you let the wet evaporate
and rinse mine in the relentless
resurrection of the hydrology.

What did the spit mean to the man
when he juiced it for the face of Jesus

or the mouthful of apple and mucus
Adam sauced and spat out onto the sod
of Eden?

            The mark, the imprimatur
of non-comprehension,
                        of refusal
turned into the religion of the road
to Arafat—
            knowledge—and the hag
it turned into on that Haj.

I spit in a cycle of response
to self-inflicted or uninvited infusoria
who reside, murky or translucently
as Lucifer, in my petty addictions
and infections.
                In the iron grating
at the kerbside, herbaceous borders,
gutters, the spontaneous spittoons
of flower pots—I leave my dollop,
like cuckoo spit on spear grass,

which we once prodded with nausea
            and fascination in our search
for sour leek to eat and sweet stems
            among the blades of grass—a rabble

of wee ruminants for the cud
        of the pre-Christian, "Pagan
parcel of wee hellions,"
            my mother called us,

who in God's good time came to the See
        of higher learning
to quarrel with the faithful.
        11+ Protestants,
who protested against all religions
        with the black pint of our perception raised
like a free Guinness.

One night, boarding a Waterworks bus,
I vented into the visage
of starry superstition off the back platform,
cocksure of the advantage
                        in my sceptic's
view, a quarrelsome agnostic, swinging
around the curve of Albert Street, I saw
the street lights as an unbroken ring
of grinding thorns
and my head broke open, poured
through bright holes in the dark

like the streetlight's drivel of illumination
onto the concrete—
my consciousness turned fluid,
                        hard
and coarse.

            My rheum, is it a quitting
            or quickening,

a condensation
of that consciousness?

The dog eats grass
and retches
a glistening bundle
of the greenery

or excretes the blades
with difficulty,
walking with its tailings
under its tail,

the impulse to purge
sticking in the process—

how revolting,
                     how sticky
in mine, I am.

Everything I use
to clear things from my mind
                     or throat
clings,
webbed in a clarity.

               A petal of spit,
a petal of electrostatic plastic

off the handle for a bag of groceries
from Safeway

I can't shake from my finger.

A daily glomming
      in the gloaming
where I spat on the countenance
      of an idea,
the face of faith
      in the half-dark
      and I swim, swim,
            walk, walk
to the end of that spittle,
           my little knowledge.

It dries
      within a breath of the desert,
      dissolves in the salt of the sea
—that Haj
      undertaken to where Cortes

at la Audencia spits on his hand
      to shake Sandoval's for a commission:

three ships to go sailing in
      on Christ's birthday, onto a shore
of the unnamed sea which will take his.

          Constantly
I fall off the Waterworks bus into his bay
of brigantines:
      Hope, Charity and Faith
that there is a landing place, a beach
      of undisturbed chocolopa,
      sitting,
      glistening
      on the burnished face of the sand

before they dissolve
            into the pores of its shifting history

where I make landfall.

        I return to the wet hull
on the spit, the vessel
        of my vision
        to ponder and to wonder
        what escapes
        and never leaves the clay
        of a man and woman's quickening,

        why matters stick to the fingers,
        why matters stray

devoted and deviant
as a child at play

hunting the incredulous creature
that forces him to expectorate
and speculate

the chocolopa

lodged like an ocean-
cuckoo
in his chest.

WHAT DO YOU CALL IT, WHAT DO YOU CALL ME, WHAT DO YOU CALL US?

> "Where he comes from,
> they played cricket
> with bricks." –Angela

"*Barley* . . . " its *e-e-e*s squeal
about the hard little cereal
in my head, like a gnat   .
or midge I can't swat

as I try to translate
the Spanish word for the soup into some sign
or significance in my reprobate
English. For—in this coarse, natural tongue of mine

there is a clear identity to the taste.
I know I learned its chaste
flavour first—
and a certain favour, even thirst

for the stuff—when cooked under brisket
in a soup; sweetened
and swollen with the meat and veg—tidbits
of parsnip, leek, and a harmony that congealed

on the musical knives and forks in my
mother's scullery,
where we ate
as humbly as servants of our great

Lord on a Sunday, too shy
or tidy to sit
by and by
at our double-leaf, wiggly-legged

table in the front room
that opened directly onto the boom
and blatter of double-decker buses or big-bosomed aunt
barging in. 'Like eating in hell's restaurant,'

my mother said, 'in the middle of that traffic!'
Distrustful of what the dark outside
might deposit in the door, I lick
my lips, and resplendent in my own sweat, preside.

More like the gleaming gristle of a clam
among an opulence of oysters than
an articulate foreigner,
I stare

across my plate in the Metropole.
This is a mystery strained from the hardness
of the whole,
through the boil and hiss

of the pot, into liquid of pearl.
The aromatic mash—peasant recipe of a Polish earl
    (could as well have had the belligerence
    of the barley dried to burn as a tight-fisted incense,

        distilled as whisky or left for our cook to harvest.)
"Cream of barley," I find it for Gabriel and Basia,
suddenly, after the longest
time, lolling on my tongue's amnesia,

or it was concussed
by synesthesias of memory, blunder-bussed
in, and the grapeshot of possibilities
killed my normal verbal agilities.

Translator, orchard-raider of vocabulary, all a-hobble
in a Polish restaurant, Mexico City, on the Calle
Amsterdam that curves in a foolish
and full circle,

and in such a fashion that people get
lost along each exit
or entrance in the memory. Where will any one
of them leave you pointed on Calle Amsterdam? At the
gun

of a robber or kidnapper,
in an endless toss of grim alternatives?
What riches can I stand and deliver?   The liquor
of an un-alcoholic barley through a sieve

of summers, when its raw stock was a little boy's
ammunition of choice
at Carnalea, where he went hunting mischief
in a field near the cliff

of adolescence. "Heel," and "Heed!"
It was a flowing pelt of chaff and wind he could command;
he even felt it, like a bristly wheaten
mongrel, sniff his hand.

Where to sic it? This way, that, and the other it wags.
Every sweep of his hand snags
more barleyed teeth to use—on whom?
Through the wood,
south, to Brown's farm he would

certainly find Jean, always the thoroughfare
to a fall over his prime precipice:
bum-embossed, primrose-embroidered.
Down its soft-bank, without a kiss

they entered a coitus of belligerence
with her cheap locket breaking,
and the barley springing from his pocket,
egging her on to root about her
and pay him back with his own shooter

in the middle of their rolls—
she could never take it! Outside the restaurant
on the Calle Amsterdam a vigilante patrols
the parked cars that haunt

young ruffians like me, who could easily have violated
these expensive harlots with red
and amber eyes,
every model with no keys

 other than the imagination in their scarred
fingers, and a prurience
bred agile on backyard
walls that grow broken glass as a subsistence

crop.
        (I lick the top
        of the spoon
        and Angela puts on a face for her baboon.)

Gabriel says even his VW Rabbit
has the knack of appearing ripe for
someone to rob it.
So he does not lock the door

to save on broken windows. The "cebada"
pauses on the tongue of a lad a
league or two away from himself,
who bought the stuff from a bin on a shelf

that stood a foot
off the floor:
tin pillar of barleys, as bald as a coots,
standing in an odour,

like wine. Inspected closely in the palm,
it was the insulting cereal simulacrum
of a head: ours, back then—shaven down to the
muscles
at the back of the skull; the skin marbled into terrify-
ing tousles

by winter light. Our barleys were
the untranslatable glee of an ancient
battle hex we spat at one another.
Through our fluent

shooters the voices spoke the platinum
and cream-coloured runes of long-dead Celts, or Nor-
dic harassers in one
mouthful. Like ours, who warred in pseudonyms as
Brits, even the narrow
straw had to borrow

a name, lumbered with the bulkiness of "pea"
we couldn't afford, or shoot hard enough, and only ate
as a delicacy, served heated up with vinegar in an ice
cream shop. The free,
hand-picked, or bought barley was an affordable hate

to spew. It loved us well as targets,
and once discharged, it
felt like it had grown through our mouths out of flag-
stones
up our road. Oh barley! Versatile weapon

or whisky. Blithe barley—this haute cuisine,
now white and cosy as the cream
of conversation, miles away from that vile little ancestry
of mine, planted in the clod of Carnalea

or fleet
fields of fertile
concrete
up the Shankill.

In our dialect, egg rhymes with *hag* and *bag*,
and to say a *hegg begg* gives
the glottal regions of the mouth and throat
great exercise, but this morning
I did arrest myself
from saying such to my wife
(who comes from a strain
of Irish with superior inflections)
just before she picked one up
(an egg). I did not let
the coarse consonance
put one over on my tongue
or the whippet in my throat
inch craftily
away from me, the one
that goes for the oral rabbit,
the juicy joints
where harsh hunger sounds
sink their teeth fast
through the soft fur
of the verb
all so the dastardly ear
can feed the fury of a mouth.

Oral rabbit, even as I think it turns
into Oral Roberts and a memory
that I was saved a hundred times over
by backstreet preachers—Baptists,
Congregationalists,
members of the Ebenezer Hall,
who would have us
put a clamp on our tongue
because of the blasphemies
and lies that fed on them. The *hegg*
would be a lie—for at that moment,
in the fridge light, I saw the morning curl

and sweep that gives daily nuance to her hair,
and middle-eastern opulence of her nose
The rudder
for the rich trading ship of her body,
once laden with eggs,
that always took me aboard
no matter what my wares
and tear-away tongue
might embark on her.

IN PLACE OF TONSILS THEY PROMISED ME A BLADDER BALL

1. The Infusion

In place of tonsils, they promised me a bladder ball.
I came home from the Ben Hospital
at Carlysle Circus to the hard brown leather
and bladder, which with my two feet I tethered
as I blew it up into a round lump
with a bicycle pump,
after stuffing it between the virgin laces.

With the first gust of air into the slack spaces
the noise from my un-tonsilled throat improved;
I hooted at the blatter and squeak
through the sac, which was folded and gloved
inside, like a squid in its hole.

My chest began to peak
on air, as if the pump's connection were a whole
other windpipe and the ball, a kick-
able lung not to risk on our waste-ground, disastrous
place for leather balls with goal post pillars of brick.

I tried to persuade my mates to hop the bus
up to Woodvale Park, where we could play
on the only lick of grass, a mile away.

The twang of ball on paving stone was the brute
music we were used to, our minstrel band;
on the other hand,
the hush of grass, the swish, the flounce
its wide acreage, a mystery to our legs, and muds,
curds of clay under it, like to lick the studs
off our football boots.

Players thighs grew like tree trunks out of that muck
into First Division dray's. Fetlocked in socks:
one of those fellas could pull a team behind them.

Up in the park pitch, no skifter of feet, *liddle*
pass, dribble on gravel, skim
over a puddle
with a perma-grey lining of kitchen flagstone
from a house floor, still there from the Blitz.

This field—once they reseeded its
fallow green with shirts, every season—
was too wide and too arable
for us, who were good and able
only to sprint over
to the bookies, between races at Doncaster,
for our parents or across the ruined square
which was our pitch and not a yard farther.

2. Disillusion

Fear and awe set in
when the time-tabled teams took over the goals
on the grass and we drifted away to kick randomly,
glancing down at where the kiln
in the brickworks roared
in a manmade gorge
along the fringes of the park.

Then, we dribbled downcast
and downhill with my ball,
now properly scratched and scored,
relegated to the lower divisions of the Shankill.
until one night in late June,
Alfie McMichael came, an archangel in slip-on shoes,
in a sports shirt and thrilling elegance of slacks

that blew around his legs
while his eyes moved among us,
like an armourer's in a munitions factory,
a sorter's over the sacks at a seed store,
picking through the dry click of feet
for the spark in our poor powder keg,
the holy grain of a goal
in the pass one of us might make.

It was like he had stepped from the back of our minds,
where he had been for seasons
and arrived
everywhere the ball was, in two steps,
just passing to us, never taking a shot;
then, through the dirty footwork
of our rubber runners he drove one.
like the 6:30 train through a station
it screeched to the opposite goal,
and hit the backyard wall
with a thud as though in the raw June sunset
the dull red blaze of still-standing bricks
on the other side of the war-destroyed
street were an affront
or abominable buffer.

I took the ball home and listened, over and over,
to the noise of his feet on the leather:
the power I wanted to route
through everything I would ever do—
kick—into the rhyme of this leather ball I have carried
puffed-up like another head
under my arm with the grit and the green
still keen, still clinging.

Your Da's a Brussel sprout
And your Ma's a cabbage.

The truck, especially
He could not disturb one nut,
One bolt in the body or operation
Of the engine. The thick
Stubbornness in the tyres,
As high as his shoulders;
The boy stands, determined
Not to move if it doesn't—parked,
There, next the hawthorn tree,
Which can't be cut without killing it
And blighting the life of the feller.
He knows the key in the starts the sparks in the ignition,
That the hawthorn depends on remaining rooted
While the treads on the tyres wind as stubbily as bark
Through the rubber.
The bed of the truck smells like a field
Of mixed wet vegetables, packets of which
He buys for his mother-made soup
When he's in Belfast.
He holds the truck in his eye;
If he does not look away,
It will stay rooted,
Like the hawthorn tree,
But the key that starts the sap
Turns inside him—how hard
To hold the truck stopped;
It's the holidays, Easter Week—
They are down from town
And Mr. Brown, the farmer, calls.
He knows the boy this long time,
"Since the truck was a twig,"
He says—like it really is a tree
And he, Farmer Brown, did go one day

To pick the perfect cabbage
To put this wee boy under.

Hopalong Cassidy—white hat,
platinum blonde hair, black
everything else: the perfectly dressed
paradox for boy's box office. Hat
and hair, the right colour
for the goodie; the rest,
a black match for the baddie.
In later life, in Mexico, in cowboy
country, I will wonder
why the *guero*, the fair-haired one's
head is rubbed by even the darkest Indio
like an Aladdin's lamp.
Why do they think of the light
only as a giver of light, when it can burn out
the eyeballs, shoot through both sockets,
till everything goes black
and you won't see
your way to set foot
in the stirrup
of an afternoon matinee
again—once the sun has shucked
your skull like a common
cockle shell
for its sweetmeat.
What do you say to the giant
heat and light utility
in the sky
about its fee of human sacrifice—
life for a life, fair trade
is no robbery? The sun
and his blonde vassals—
the Viking beard in the stone,
at Tulum, stylized

like an Abyssinian god's—
where I imagine them
the city's rune
and ruin. They came, murdered
all the mighty of the Maya,
but unlike Cortés
and his conquistadors,
left—those good bad guys,
those sea-pokes,
in the ten gallon helmets
of hair—
who did not burn their boats.

HOPALONG ANGEL

by Vinicius de Moraes

From a Didi pass, *Garrincha moves upfield,
He dribbles past one, dribbles past two, then takes a short
Breather—the leather glued to his foot, eyes peeled,
As if measuring the moment for his dart.

Look at the telepathy: he slips
With greater speed than thought itself, and ease,
Dribbles past one, past another. The ball skips
Blithely from foot to foot, rooted on the breeze.

In one single spasm, the crowd goes
Contrite, rises and howls from its death throes
Its hymn of hope in unison.

Garrincha, the angel, hears and heeds: —goooooal!
It's image, a perfect cartoon: a G that shoots an O
That makes a 1 out of a zero. It's sheer juju, son.

*Garrincha was a Brazilian footballer born with one leg shorter
than the other.

MATTINS

Complacencies of the peignoir, and late
Coffee and oranges in a sunny chair,
And the green freedom of a cockatoo
Upon a rug mingle to dissipate
The holy hush of ancient sacrifice.
—Wallace Stevens' "Sunday Morning."

Out of a fold of flesh or two
rolled one hundred and four years of us:
father, mother, sons and a daughter;
time—like a crab apple, tucked
into a potato farl—was eaten
on a Sunday morning, spilling
from the mouth of the century,
tarty and unexpected, flavoured
with their lives and mine: two fathers,
a daughter, and two sons; one Douey,
three McWhirters and the Mammy, a McConnell—
our family algebra, like a riddle on a griddle—
these were the true concomitants, the menu
in our skin-bound *Book of Common Prayer*, tea
and potato farl,
together on Northumberland Street;
the brother, Ernie Douey, always edgy
to be going up to Minnie's ministrations
in the kitchen, the clutter and clatter
of her distaste at having to put a hand
to a pan, but that was her instrument of choice,
which she played loudly like a cast iron drum
till the abuse made the sausage skins split
and run black along the cicatrice.
And my own mother
made soup so thick with brisket
sappers could have swung pontoon bridges
across it, for access to the other side,

which I suppose was heaven,
already there, in our gubs. Time tells in the amputation
of our taste, a loss of faith in the suet,
sausage and the brisket, ours growing too astute
for the comforts of such communion,
the tasty and savoury dear-departed remains
cooked into a Shepherd's pie on Monday,
to take us through the week. Jesus,
those days,
our little drool and dribble of history
made one hell of a host, did it not?

Now, let us say our
Nunc Dimittis.

EVERY CITY IN THE EMPIRE

Had its set of glorious battle
Streets: Blenheim, Waterloo,
Trafalgar. In Belfast
They were, by irony
Of history, on the Falls—the Roman
Catholic and Republican road,
thoroughly English in its name—
thoroughly English names.
Queen Victoria's Albert
gave his moniker
To one of that road's widest
And on the Protestant and loyalist
Shankill (Irish for church on the hill),
There was Berlin, (very wide),
and Percy (just as broad)
Agnes, Northumberland,
Dundee, Aberdeen
and Orney, a confused mix of girth,
Orney, so narrow
I believed, you could pull
A chicken down it
And the bird would come
Out, plucked,
In the infamous Nick,
Ready for the pot
Always boiling
On that hob of hell.

A poet, Ciaran Carson, from Raglan
Street on the Falls
Said he had a nightmare
Of waking up on the Shankill.
I told him on Northumberland Street
I lived his nightmare for him.

WHERE KITS SITS

down wide Waterloo,
there is water. Two
waters in its name,
the English/French
water/l'eau
meaning the same,
makes it a double
broad boulevard
to the boats.
Always a bow
or a prow—
crude oxidized cliff
of a freighter,
or gay white cruise
ship—at the bottom.
The space of its name
amplified by the nearby
narrowness of Blenheim
and Trafalgar.
As if the streets
matched the margin
or nature
of those victories: Blenheim
goes on and on
to the great Fraser River;
Waterloo gets cut off
by an embankment at 16th
Avenue. Closer
to the water, the fusiliers
camouflaged
in its horse chestnuts
pop
periodic rounds
of fat, barbed green

buckshot,
at the inhabitants,
who have lived and died
in the house to house advance
of wood, stucco and brick,
where a great war is won
every day for the water
view.

TOWARD A DATE AT THE TONIC CINEMA

Black bats convene under the railway arches,
and lime licks curl from the damp mortar
and the joins of stones. We brought our faces together
to owls' oratorios in the beech wood. Stiff marches

by crows, black as peelers' boots in Carson's copse.
We trespassed under the glare of those aerial cops,
and the sun sank between bars of bark and moss
like the heart into a winter lock-up of Eros.

Tar between concrete slabs of the road, rusted iron ribs
under a shock of flat cement, our stiff arms, our fibs
about the kiss while a top coat kept your bosom buried in
dull brown wool, deeper than in any coffin.

Our faces touched, floating atop our clothes—drowned
fish that passed each other in a river, as unawarely,
as cavalierly cold as the horsy classes, who swooned
over dung and saddle soap, cavalry twill and camel hair

rode through Carson's, owners of copse and coppers
who patrolled us, cleaned up to look like proper
little Brits, who only embraced in the foyer of sex
before the big picture welled with its bloody loyalist hex.

PENSÉE POÉME ASSAY FOR MY SISTER

1.

When the first ecumenical motions were made toward sitting down at the same table in the sixties, my sister said the argument prone and various character of the churches was like the personalities of the twelve apostles, cooking up opinions for Jesus, over dinner. She said that when she set down a pot of marrow bone stew on the heat mat and left the ladle in, for us to help ourselves.

She must have loved that; there were a dozen and more of us, under twenty, and tucking in at Carnalea, where the family spent summers together under the one roof and in two sittings at the one deal table for every meal of the day.

Loved it until I blurted out of a full mouth, "Thirteen," and she looked at me as if she knew that—and I was the thirteenth, but she, too polite to pass the remark.

Obviously, we conducted a hearty dialectic.

When in Belfast, with my bum on the Devon grate as they called it . . . a single unit—tiled fire and mantelpiece—with an iron, overnight burner for coal at its hub. The clock sat on the middle of the mantle, to the right of my head when I discussed St. Paul, or one of the big Christian arguers, with her standing in front of me, arms folded, as if she had backed me into the fire of these inquisitions and I hadn't taken the pew there of my own sweet will.

One day we were disputing the nature of Jesus again, and I was heavy into him as the carrier of ideas. A braniac, they would call him nowadays, and that was how I fancied myself then, too.

Disgusted, she says, "You know some people say he was a homosexual," inferring that brainy men and homosexuals went together, like the Greeks. Or my lot up at Queen's University. "Queee . . . n's Univers-tity," she would say.

"Homosexual . . . isn't that queer," says I. "Some people even claim he was the son of God. "

She would have burned the house down around me for besting her, but she was of the order of the third nipple and always on the lookout with her extra eye.

2.

So you see my sister was a Celtic Christian case of a
Cassandra. She had a vision at the beginning of the
war, in 1939, a cross passed over the face of the moon.
At one point in that lunar crossing the T joint must
have reached the axes in the midnight circle, normally,
a site symbolizing the sacred round of the Celtic sun on
churches and gravestones.

The city will be crucified, she said, and dragged her
nearest the twelve miles from Belfast down to the sum-
mer bungalow at Carnalea, whose asbestos walls would
do better against fire than against the cold winter.

But there we stayed until the bombs were done and we
came back to the incendiary smell that had got under
the wallpaper and been kilned into the bricks. Loose
ones of which we tossed, neighbour boy at neighbour
boy, adding our bellicose reassembly of the houses to
the blitz's.

We gathered right off that houses are explodeable,
then recyclable as weapons. We only needed new war
to break out again, and it did—after waiting faithfully
for us to attend to demolitions, as we surely would.
Her formerly unexcitable sister-in-law ducking in be-
hind the door to sit on the chair that was always there,
declaring, They almost got me that time, till she died
of a stroke; or the snipers drawing beads on her neph-
ew, who climbed down his fireman's ladder to report,
closehand, on the damage due to erupt and the disrup-
tion done—she saw it all coming around the corner of
her third eye, except this time, when what she forecast
lying ahead in the way of bad omens was a squadron of
our own flyboys, she refused to get out of the road.

FOR MY SHANKILL ROAD SISTER

She had a bosom and biceps that could have burst
chains of Sheffield steel, but could not break the link
between her and that corner of the Shankill she came
from,

like the cells in her cervix that killed her,
locked and growing as uncontainably wild inside her
as her belief in God
or her temper.

I like to think of her in her moment of salvation,
in the other cell she loved and laboured over
like her own womb. That built-on kitchen
and bathroom with an enamel tub
at the back of her kitchen house—
mini-fridge, immersion heater—

3 Craig's Terrace.

Some of our ones, Protestants in a fast car, had done
the typical
and terrible down on the Falls Road and were being
chased
by the Paras and the RUC up onto the Shankill via
Northumberland Street,
where I used to live, and which connected Shankill
and Falls—
another killer link or open thoroughfare(take your pick)
between our opposite religions or diseases,
which we can't outlive or break.
To take a short cut, and block the cops and Paras
from coming in behind them into Craig's Terrace,

our ones tossed a bomb from the car.
Down came the houses
on either side; my sister—on hers—
felt the concussion of the blast in her face,
saw the walls of her kitchen heave, their red brick lining
shift. And she stepped back,
opened the door to the yard behind her,
stepped out
and back until her kitchen and bathroom
and everything she loved
lay piled at her feet. But she was safe.

I wish she could have stepped out
from inside her other cell, safe
to her own regenerate from degenerate self. But none
of us can do that yet,
can we?
God bless you, Lily.

Born in 1939 in Belfast, Northern Ireland, **George Mc-Whirter** grew up on the Shankill Road. He attended Queen's University in Belfast, where his classmates included Seamus Heaney, and later completed a Masters degree at the University of British Columbia. McWhirter lived in Spain from 1965 to 1966, when he moved to Canada where he taught high school in Port Alberni, making an abrupt transition from Barcelona to living in a log cabin by Sproat Lake. He is the author of twenty books, many of which have won major awards, including the Commonwealth Poetry Prize, the MacMillan Prize for Poetry, the Canadian Chapbook Poetry Competition Winner, the Ethel Wilson Fiction Prize, and the FR Scott Prize for Translation. In 2005, George Mc-Whirter retired as a professor in the Creative Writing Department at UBC. In 2007 he was inaugurated as the first Poet Laureate for the City of Vancouver.